GREATEST OF MEN
WASHINGTON

"the Purest Figure of History."
GLADSTONE.

BY

ALFRED W. McCANN, LL.D.
AUTHOR OF "GOD—OR GORILLA"

WIPF & STOCK · Eugene, Oregon

Wipf and Stock Publishers
199 W 8th Ave, Suite 3
Eugene, OR 97401

Greatest of Men Washington
By McCann, Alfred W.
ISBN 13: 978-1-5326-1794-2
Publication date 2/17/2017
Previously published by
The Devin-Adair Company, 1927

DEDICATION

To May, true woman; to the immortal spirit of Frances; to Muriel, alias "Patsy"; to "Al" and Rosemary and Justin, alias Jake; to the three Pauls; to George and Hank and Austin; to Jack, and "Des," Mary Angela and Denise; to "Ken" and Junior, Kathleen and Jane; to Betty and Virginia, Harry and "Den"; to Helen, Louise and "Skeezicks"; to Newman, Arty, Jimmy and Buddy; to Eleanor and Katherine and the "Twins"; to Frank and Bill and Val, and to the two "Bobbies," and to all the young people of the world that they too may be, in their time, true women and true men.

THE AUTHOR.

PREFACE

THE romantic daring of sentimentalists and the commercial daring of belittlers, coming at last together like two fog-banks, threaten to envelop a figure whose true proportions America can ill afford to view vaguely. A blurred vision of Washington is no vision at all. Out of one fog "he hurls a stone over the Palisades," "heaves a floundered cart from ditch to road-bed," "pins a blustering wrestler's shoulders to the earth," accepts "a laurel wreath from Destiny." Astonishing! Trivial! But happily transparent.

It is the other fog that matters. Under its cover Washington has been given a beggar's body haunted by bad dreams and a little world to move in, scarcely larger than a nut-shell, filled with lethal gas. The issue has ceased to be trivial. It is no longer transparent. One is unable to see through it at a glance.

Between the old apocryphal and the new cubistic images stalks an immense distortion benign at one extreme, malignant at the other. The power of malice increases geometrically with the elegance of its grooming. Rhetorically gowned and culturally bur-

PREFACE

nished it becomes an ingratiating force travelling in the livery of "Good." Its chariot is always "Truth"; its objective the "emancipation of mankind from the shackles of error, superstition and make-believe."

So the "real Washington" is stripped of all the trappings of a "maudlin century" and shown "as he was"—for assassination. None may recognize the apparition, but the glimpse, for the thing is clearly labelled "Washington," is enough to bring Illusion to its knees. The myth becomes an effigy; the effigy a man; the man a little less than casual—a person. Why preserve him at all? Let him go!

The whole process of assault, involving high praise, has been insidious, subtle and—tremendously effective. Butchery, if it be artistic, is so essentially modern that not one in ten thousand will challenge the motive or the deed. True the "age of reason" challenges everything, but in challenging everything it challenges nothing. This was sometime a paradox, but now the time gives it proof. Why should not Washington sprawl where the butchers have felled him?

There is no Antony to read his will. Who, indeed, will read the tens of thousands of pages of letters, manuscripts, state papers, reports, account books, diaries and contemporary records? Who will check the "new" against the true? Who will care in this busy, this almost crazy, life of tension,

PREFACE

bombarded by a thousand thundering distractions, to seek out a mere man among the dead? It isn't done, and no man will do it—except in love.

But perhaps a million men will read something to the point—if it be brief enough—something that will fling the false against the half-true; the spurious against the fiction. After all, it is so easy to find the real Washington, and to wish to guide a neighbor to his shrine smacks so of the badge and ceremony of presumption, that only an extraordinary occurrence can justify another addition to the Mt. Vernon shelves. But love, mixed with indignation, will eagerly stoop to any folly.

Hence in these short chapters the idly curious, the new iconoclasts, the ultra-sophists, the super-critics and the "old adorers" will find cross-examination and rebuttal, evidence and summation. The real Washington is here! The Washington of proof is here! Fresh contrasts and startling contradictions are here; all the half-truths broken into bits; the whole falsehoods dissolved in lye!

"For it is, as the air, invulnerable,
And our vain blows malicious mockery."

In the meantime we are not self-deceived by any hope that what we have done may survive its hour. As portrait it possesses scar and mole. As a lyric it is without music. As an epic it lacks every tower

PREFACE

and pinnacle from whose tops heroic trumpets blare. But as a close-up of a living being, a hand-clasp with Washington himself, it may be welcomed by countless thousands for its verity and warmth. The author's one hope is that it may bring refreshment to the thirsting and throbbing heart of youth for it is the likeness of a **MAN**!

CONTENTS

CHAPTER	PAGE
I.—Two Little Men with Quills	3
II.—Beguiling Belindas	10
III.—The Secret Love Letters	17
IV.—The Sally Fairfax Scandal	25
V.—An Astounding Puzzle	33
VI.—Four Philandering Epistles	38
VII.—Stupidity! Cruelty!! Slaves!!!	46
VIII.—Idealist or Turnip Sower	51
IX.—Hard Drink and Gambling	56
X.—Fox-Hunting and Dinners	61
XI.—All Off to the Races	66
XII.—Braggadocio at Its Worst	71
XIII.—Imperious Egotism	76
XIV.—Dull, Sullen, Gloomy, Grave	81
XV.—A Grand Opera General	86
XVI.—Absurd Antics on the Delaware	94
XVII.—British and Jesuit Calumnies	100

CONTENTS

CHAPTER	PAGE
XVIII.—UTTERLY DEVOID OF SENTIMENT	105
XIX.—WHAT THEY CALL TOASTING	111
XX.—CONTEMPT FOR THE POPULACE	116
XXI.—INCONSIDERATE, IMPERIOUS	122
XXII.—MADEIRA, PORT AND RHENISH	127
XXIII.—THE SPIRIT OF THE TAVERN	132
XXIV.—PAID FOR IN MONEY	137
XXV.—THE COLD AND SILENT MAN	142
XXVI.—AN EPIC OF HATRED	147
XXVII.—WASHINGTON'S ILLITERACY	153
XXVIII.—THE MARY PHILIPSE SCANDAL	158
XXIX.—VANITY AND BIGOTRY	166
XXX.—WASHINGTON'S LOVE OF WASHINGTON	173
XXXI.—WASHINGTON'S COLDNESS TO HIS MOTHER	180
XXXII.—A MYTH CANNOT CREATE	187
XXXIII.—WASHINGTON'S IRISH PREJUDICE	192
XXXIV.—BURNING THE POPE IN FIRE	199
XXXV.—WASHINGTON THE UN-AMERICAN	206
XXXVI.—OTHER UN-AMERICAN AMERICANS	213
XXXVII.—WASHINGTON AND THE TERROR	218
XXXVIII.—WASHINGTON THE INFIDEL	227

CONTENTS

CHAPTER	PAGE
XXXIX.—THE MISCHIEF OF HIS YOUTH	235
XL.—WASHINGTON AND THE MOB	241
XLI.—OF FLESH AND FAITH	246
XLII.—WHO'S WHO IN AMERICA	252
XLIII.—WASHINGTON AND YOUTH	258
XLIV.—WASHINGTON—THE MAN'S MAN	266

Greatest of Men—Washington

Greatest of Men—Washington

CHAPTER I

TWO LITTLE MEN WITH QUILLS

BLUNTLY! George Washington was the most consummate hypocrite, mountebank and adventurer the world has ever known, or he was one of the noblest and purest creatures who have ever lived in any land or any age. In support of one contention we have much whispering, astonishingly recent in origin, full-grown at birth, with no ancestors to explain its coming into the world. At the other extreme we have established truths that will survive the scrutiny of any supreme court on earth.

Between 1759 and 1774 two letters, "G. W.," were sufficient to open all doors in Virginia. From 1774 to 1799 they opened all doors in America. In 1889 a feeble effort was made to put them in lower case— "g. w." In 1926 a new brand of courage appeared in the world. Two little men with fountain pens restored the upper case, but made it read "Godless!" "Wanton!"

GREATEST OF MEN—WASHINGTON

Camel prints in the desert, rain marks on the ridge, mists at the base of a mountain are unhappily not like the voices of two little men. Obliterated by drifting sands, wiped out by passing winds, dissolved by sunlight, these faint phenomena imperceptibly disappear as humanity, discerning their just proportions, briefly notices and goes upon its way.

Alas, not so evanescent are the voices of two little men. Little voices do not play upon the desert, the ridge, or the granite peak. Falling upon little minds, like their own, they produce effects stupendously out of proportion to their littleness. Perhaps they catch the ear of iconoclastic youth. Youth is prone to believe. Gray beards are not immune. So, two little voices, commanding two little fountain pens, may indeed become objects of concern. To notice them is to grant their one desire. To let them go unnoticed is to concede the very point they would make.

The defendant who refuses to take the witness stand may create a doubt where there is none. Hence, in this world, the rôle of attested truth.

George Washington was, after all, a rather Interesting Animal, little more. Agreeable revelation to men surfeited with scandal. One more reason for throwing the harness off. What can be more consoling to conscience than the discovery that a

TWO LITTLE MEN WITH QUILLS

creature pictured as eminently noble is only so much meat? It is bad enough when the world-weary become cynics, but the nation whose youth are taught cynicism contemplates disaster.

Perhaps it is well for the 1926 biographers that Washington is dead. Roosevelt could carry his libellers into court. The son of Gladstone, who describes Washington as "the purest figure of history," could meet his father's assailant in the presence of wig and gown. But the 1926 detractors need not fear civil or criminal action. The dead are without redress.

So to the truth. Was Washington, as a youngling, the plaything of depravity, a philanderer, an ungrateful, unfilial and unfeeling son? Was his mother an inferior woman?

Washington's home life, it is hinted, was an outwardly smooth veneer covering a hidden affliction. Not only was he an unfaithful husband, but there is an innuendo to the effect that the curse of disease was in his flesh.

Addicted to alcohol and cards, this hard drinking gambler and frivolous flirt was a skilled liar, a land speculator, an adventurer, an overdressed marionette laced and frilled like a popinjay. The cold-blooded, unsentimental, prosaic, non-imaginative hybrid of gentleman and farmer was an investment-patriot. There is paradox here, but there is more.

GREATEST OF MEN—WASHINGTON

What appeared to be patriotism was the greed of a shrewd and selfish nature. He was not a statesman, but he did possess craft in getting rid of sick or crippled slaves, first by lashing and then by dispatching them to an island hell. He estimated human life cheaply and had a profound contempt for the populace. He furnished a pot overflowing with scandal.

These lights come by revelation. Illuminating the new portrait, they help us model in spotted clay a clumsy reconstruction of a Thing which might well be named the American Pithecanthropus Erectus. Caricature is neither fair nor true biography. Francis X. Talbot calls it an utter distortion of viewpoint.

What a pity the iconoclasts are not interested in the ordinary little things of human existence. Strangely indeed are the hidden ways of life revealed. A study of Washington among the Indians, at Mt. Vernon, in the saddle, on his farms, in the inns and taverns of his day, at his writing-table making entries in his diary, is the study of America from Washington's boyhood to his grave.

The truth it brings to the surface is priceless, for it gives us the habits and customs of America in the making and also in photographic detail the simple splendor of a man.

Never was self-revelation more unconsciously ex-

TWO LITTLE MEN WITH QUILLS

hibited; never was defamation more effectively riddled.

In all four volumes of his diary, written for no eyes but his own, and until 1925 published only in shreds and patches, there is not one entry of coarseness, not a word that can be garbled by a specialist in littleness, meanness, barrenness to put a prop under the thing he looks for.

At the age of twenty-one, twenty miles down the Ohio, treating with the Half-King Tanacharison he conveyed to his diary what the Indian said. For sheer nobility of sentiment there is nothing finer in American literature than the narrative of this immature lad.

At the age of forty-seven he wrote from West Point to the president of the Congress: "I shall never palliate my own faults by exposing those of another."

These are two milestones separating the youthful Washington from the mature. What lies between is just as simple, high-minded and human as either extreme. What came after will leave him who attempts to follow it all the richer for his journey.

We are not interested in the candied stuff spooned out to lovers of sweetmeats. The cherry-tree story cloys and sickens just as the nauseating pills of the pathologist make sorrowful him who is asked to swallow. The cherry tree episode may have occurred. The story may be true, but—it can't be proved. What we want is proof.

To know Washington, so unlike either of the extremes portrayed by canonizer and defamer, one must have breakfast with him, mount one of his horses, and never leave his side. In such intimacy not alone what he says is eloquent and revealing, but what it never occurs to him to say is far more so.

Perhaps no man ever saw a canvas of High Romance framed in common spruce until George Washington, ignorant of what he was doing, manifested himself to his fellows. Surely nothing is more startling in the history of the human race than the poverty of vainglory in the heart of this man.

Not once does his diary exult over an enemy. Nowhere does it contain a triumphant word. The canard to the effect that he was given to violent rages and tempests of passion is blasted by the utter tranquillity of his temper when he sets down the record of a trying or difficult circumstance. Expecting frailty from human nature he does not storm when he comes upon it.

Plunging with him into the forests, following him over the old countryside, lodging with him overnight at ordinaries, dining with him on the way, spending week-ends with him at Mt. Vernon, is to see him as he was and to discover how the people

TWO LITTLE MEN WITH QUILLS

lived in those stirring days, how they bled and suffered and triumphed over odds, the like of which are not now to be found in the whole world.

So we start out together.

CHAPTER II

BEGUILING BELINDAS

OUR first peep at George Washington as a boy is invited by himself, when at the age of sixteen, March 16, 1748, while surveying a tract of land lying on Cates Marsh and Long Marsh he writes this at Frederick Town:

"We cleaned ourselves to get Rid of y. Game we had catched y. night before . . . and had a good Dinner prepar'd for us. Wine Rum Punch in Plenty and a good Feather Bed with clean Sheets which was a very agreeable regale."

March 31, 1748, he assists in the eating of two wild turkeys. He is just a boy with a healthy appetite. The first American inn he mentions (April 12, 1748), is West's Ordinary, at the head of the Bull Run Mountain. He is interested in stumps, courses and distances, and loves to camp without a cloth upon the table. When he shoots twice at wild birds but kills *none* he says so. He simply can't invent an exploit. He is his own cook. His spits are forked sticks, his plates are large chips. Dishes he has none.

BEGUILING BELINDAS

But he knows contrasts. At nineteen, November 10, 1751, accompanying his tubercular and dying brother in the latter's search for health at Barbados, he writes:

"After Dinner was the greatest Collection of Fruit I have yet seen on the Table there was Granadella the Sappadilla Pomgranate Sweet Orange Water Lemon forbidden Fruit apples Guaves &ca. &ca. &ca."

His spelling is youthfully phonetic. It will be improved, rapidly. Little men will seize upon the earlier flaws and offer them as proof that Washington was illiterate.

These little men, exhibiting themselves as masters of letters, must therefore accuse Shakespeare's illiteracy or confess an ignorance of Shakespeare incompatible with their own scholarly pretensions. Washington was a better speller than Shakespeare. His use of capital letters and punctuation marks was obviously based upon the Shakespearean model.

One of the troubles of the little men arises in rashness. Having never seen any edition of Shakespeare except such as have been carefully corrected by editors, they are obviously not aware that the First Folio of 1623 shockingly betrays the "illiteracy" of the author of "Hamlet" and "The Tempest." If Washington's very good spelling makes him illiterate, to what state of savagery does Shakespeare's very bad spelling reduce the pride and glory of English letters?

Back to Washington's youth. He notes that his companions are "the most kind and friendly." This comment is scarcely to be characterized as a response to viciousness. All its companion comments are so youthful, so homely and so wholesome, so natural and unaffected. The boy has no conceit. Attending a play, he reports not what he thinks of its merits, but rather the opinion of those better qualified to judge. "The character of Barnwell and several others *was said* to be well performed." Even at this early date the justice and moderation of his decisions, in matters however trifling, and his scrupulous devotion to exact truth are foreshadowings of the man to come. A petty though eloquent incidence of his heroic accuracy is found in two deleted words in the paragraph introducing Martha's expenses from Virginia to his winter quarters. You will discover this for yourself a little later.

Two days after the play, November 17, 1751, he "Was strongly attacked with the small Pox." There is no self-pity for his misfortune. It is just an occurrence in his life and what he discovers of human nature fills him with gratitude. Deeply impressed by "the very constant attendance of Dr. Lanahan" until his recovery and "the kindness of Major Clark's family who visited me in my illness

BEGUILING BELINDAS

and contributed all they could in sending me the necessaries required in ye disorder," he makes an imperishable record of his thanks.

He is now convalescing, December, 1751, in Barbados. He should be interested in beguiling Belindas but his thoughts are strangely out of keeping with the conduct of a gay adventurer. He is admiring the governor of Barbados for "living a retired life at little expense as a gentleman of good sense."

He notes the wisdom of this man in "avoiding the errors of his predecessors," and observes that while "giving no handle for complaint his declining much familiarity makes him not overzealously beloved."

He studies fruits, specially the pineapple, China orange and Avacado pear, expressing partiality for the pine. He studies the quality of the rich black soil and compares it with the richest Marsh Mould back home. He studies the quantity of sugar to the acre, and marvels "how wonderful it is that such people should be in debt and not be able to indulge themselves in the necessaries of life." Every gentleman exhibits hospitality and a genteel behavior to the stranger but the ladies, while very agreeable, are, by ill-custom or what-not, given to affectation.

Here is Lothario indeed, a scandal-mongering scamp, a snippy boy of nineteen seeing life through the eye of a philosopher of forty.

Christmas Day, 1751, and the three days follow-

GREATEST OF MEN—WASHINGTON

ing, he is aboard ship in a pleasant and moderate sea dining on Irish goose, English beef, Bristol tripe, Irish ling and potatoes, all very fine, and one health to his absent friends. There is no terrific storm; no youthful exaggeration. The captain does not say, "Never have I seen such a sea!"

He has now come of age and is a major. Though but twenty-one, Governor Dinwiddie of Virginia selects him for his daring and sanity to visit and deliver a letter to the commandant of the French forces on the Ohio. The simple narrative of this adventure, written in Washington's own hand, is rich in drama without a hero; richer still in dignity and wisdom. The expedition for the most part is accomplished on foot, through rain and snow, in midwinter, across the Allegheny Mountains. There are no roads through the wilderness. Many mires and swamps lay in the way. Streams are to be forded, trees felled for the making of rafts. The sufferings of an intensely cold winter, without shelter, are paralleled by the perils of hostile Indians.

The young man has tied himself up in a Match Coat (made of skin). There is a gun in his hand, an axe in his belt, and a pack at his back. His papers are light, his provisions heavy. He has one companion, Captain Gist. For twenty-three days the two men struggle against the elements. A French Indian, fifteen steps off, fires "but fortu-

BEGUILING BELINDAS

nately missed." What does Washington say? "Washington held human life cheaply." He will dispatch the enemy. The caricature would be a poor one otherwise. But he does nothing of the kind. He writes in his diary:

"We took this fellow into custody and kept him until about 9 o'clock at night, then let him go and walked all the remaining part of the night without making any stop that we might get the start so far as to be out of the reach of their pursuit the next day, since we were well assured they would follow our track as soon as it was light."

Washington states the case in the most casual manner. He says nothing about himself. But Captain Gist also keeps a diary; also reports the attempted shooting. How does his entry square with Washington's? He says:

"The Indian made a stop and turned about. The major saw him point his gun toward us and fire. Said the major: 'Are you shot?' 'No,' said I. Upon this the Indian ran forward to a big standing white oak and went to loading his gun, but we were soon with him. I would have killed him, but the major would not suffer me to kill him."

So, on the testimony of an eye-witness, though Washington says nothing about it himself, we learn that Washington, age twenty-one, refuses to kill a would-be assassin, preferring to fix his compass, set his course, and travel all night. No fuss, no he-

GREATEST OF MEN—WASHINGTON

roics, no philosophizing, no moralizing, no boasting. The incident occurred and that is the end of it. Nearly thirty years later the same George Washington refuses to shoot the traitor, General Charles Lee, whom he is content, after courtmartialling, to let out of the army in disgrace.

Back to the youth. He is now twenty-two (1754) and is on the march with two Companies of Foot. One has to read carefully to realize that he is in action against the French. The big, powerful, competent boy-man is actually shy in setting forth any achievement in which he has a hand.

He is now a lieutenant-colonel. The French are outraging the borderers. With eighteen pieces of cannon, sixty bateaux, 300 canoes and a thousand men they drive from their post a group of settlers from Virginia, Maryland and England, gathered together as part of the Ohio Company.

Washington will now have his hands full. Incidentally he will ripen ten years in one. June 6, 1754, he is saddened to learn of "the death of *poor* Colonel Fry." By Fry's death his own rank is advanced. He will now be Colonel Washington, age twenty-two. That one word "poor" is rich indeed. There are no gestures of sorrow, but who will say that hypocrisy, concealed indifference, pretended sentiment hide under such a monosyllable in such a place?

CHAPTER III

THE "SECRET" LOVE LETTERS

WASHINGTON is now twenty-six. The two books published 1926 dealing with his "love affairs" are so contradictory with respect to the Sally Fairfax romance that either both should be read in deadly parallel, or neither read at all. Washington is accused of carrying on a "secret" correspondence with the wife of his dearest friend. He is aflame with volcanic fire which he cannot control.

"He was not criminal enough to leave her letters lying about, but she had old garrets and trunks in which to hide his. She could read them stealthily and gloat over what she knew (secretly) of the man whom the world, even of England, had come to accept as the greatest, noblest of his time—or, perhaps, of all time."

So concludes one of the authors.

That Sally Fairfax's priceless letters are not to be found is explained by the suggestion that perhaps Washington did not dare keep them. "He was probably accused of being a fickle lover who, goaded by her taunting irony, made an outcry of frenzy, a pitiful confession," a cad-like betrayal of his own Martha. Notice the "probably."

The other author hazards a chivalric hint. He says: "Mrs. Sally Fairfax was probably a woman of virtue." Regretting the chivalry and the "probably" he promptly adds: "Though the extremely slippery nature of this quality (virtue) always gives it an air of uncertainty." Resuming the rôle of gallantry, he goes on:

"I think that Washington had been in love with her from the time he first met her, but had never told her so. She was his friend's wife; and that alone, unless I am greatly in error as to his character, would have prevented him from revealing his affection in any definite manner."

So at the very point where one assails Washington the other defends him, though in the abyss of paradoxes all defense becomes assault.

What are the facts? At the time the "incriminating" letter was written Washington was twenty-six years old and unmarried, though engaged to the young widow Martha Custis, of whose four children two delicate tots remained alive to be subsequently fathered and loved by the man who from that time and for forty-three years thereafter wore about his neck, suspended from a gold chain, a miniature portrait of their mother.

THE "SECRET" LOVE LETTERS

Washington did write Sally Fairfax, who was having his shirts made for him. "The shirt fits tolerably well," he assures her, but suggests that the others be made with somewhat narrower wristbands. In this "secret" correspondence he begs her to make his compliments to her sister and to Miss Nancy West. Please remember also that Sally's own blood and Washington's were mingled through the marriage of a sister and a brother. They could scarcely have been closer.

Another "secret" letter to the wife of his friend begs her to give his compliments to Miss Hannah and Miss Dent. This "secret" letter is carried to her by his own brother. Never were letters more innocent.

One of them, the deadly one, dated "Camp at Fort Cumberland, 12th September, 1758," ends with this secret: "Col. Mercer, to whom I delivered your message and compliments, joins me very heartily in wishing you and the Ladies of Belvoir the perfect enjoyment of every happiness the world affords." This is remarkable evidence of *"secret"* correspondence. Col. Mercer is not out of the secret. The ladies of Belvoir are obviously in the secret. Nevertheless it's a "stealthy, gloating" business and must be so regarded.

Martha Washington knew all about Sally Fairfax. They visited continuously between Mt. Vernon and Belvoir. Their husbands went fox-hunting together; played loo and whist in each other's libraries. When Col. Fairfax moved to England, taking his wife with him, Washington managed his affairs at home.

Thirty years later Washington is still carrying on a correspondence with Mrs. Sally Fairfax, and it is Martha Washington whose quill pen puts her husband's dictation into letters as she sits at the table and tells what is going on in the neighborhood of Alexandria.

In June, 1786, Washington writes Sally's husband, assuring him that the seeds of trees and shrubs which Sally is to send him from England will remind him of the happy moments he has spent in conversations on this and other subjects with her in the old days at Belvoir. This to her own husband.

But what about the devastating letter—the letter that has brought the roof of heaven tumbling down upon the head of the greatest man America has ever seen? The iconoclasts dug this letter from the files of the New York Herald, March 30, 1877. It had been published as additional evidence of the stately character of Washington even in his lovemaking. The letter was offered for sale, at auction, by Bangs & Co., New York City, the afternoon of March 30.

THE "SECRET" LOVE LETTERS

The Herald of March 31 reports the sale as scheduled. Two letters of Washington were sold; one for $13, the other for $11.50. The names of the purchasers are not revealed. Nobody knows where the originals can be found, or indeed whether there ever was an original. The alleged newspaper copy which no living man has ever seen is remarkable for its innocence. It is not written in Washington's style. Its spelling is not his. Its punctuation belongs to another. Whether the actual writing was in Washington's hand or whether it was spurious, like the other English forgeries published during his lifetime, will never be known.

It was first referred to by Constance Carey Harrison, in Scribner's Monthly for July, 1876, under the caption "A Little Centennial Lady." The author ends her article with this violently scandalous paragraph:

"We could wish that there had been more to tell of her camaraderie with Washington. It touches one to think of the great Leader so willing to be led by the hand of a little child. It may be, that they are friends now in the presence of Him in whose sight a thousand years are but as a day."

This paragraph has no bearing upon the Sally letter but it does reveal the state of mind in which the Sally letter reposed. There was no thought of scandal, then!

GREATEST OF MEN—WASHINGTON

But, let us assume that the young bachelor did write a letter in tender terms to the woman he had known as a young girl, and between whom and him, though she were now the wife of his dear friend, there had been an enthusiastic relationship mutually exhibited, but so entirely chaste, Washington uses the word himself, and so characteristically shy that both had been almost unnaturally restrained, each yielding to admiration and deep feeling, but respecting and regretting the other's coldness, or that which through concealed sentiment appeared to be coldness.

The youth of twenty had exhibited deep feeling for "Miss Betsy," the Lowland beauty, but could never declare it because he "would only get a denial." The youth of twenty had been dumb indeed, and dumb he remained until the impulsive revelation of long smothered attachment—a revelation for which he repented through an entire lifetime thereafter in scores of letters, dwelling upon his happiness with the woman he subsequently married, and filled with his love for her children, whom he ever regarded as his own. It was a strange sin and a stranger repentance, because these letters were written not only to Sally, *but to her husband*.

Betsy, the Lowland beauty, possessed his fancy as a youth. As a boy-man Sally tormented his heart. but upon Martha, the widow, was visited all that the

THE "SECRET" LOVE LETTERS

mature Washington could give in devotion, honor, fidelity and love.

Press strongly for the genuineness of the Sally Fairfax letter, accept it for just what it is, tie it up with the forty-one years that follow. What do we get? A heroic figure rapidly stripping from his youth the pretty sentimentalities with which youth is ever aglow—a heroic figure striding, even before he has found himself, into a world of reality and substance, virtue and lofty purpose, strength of resolution, tranquil tenderness of heart.

Having come to full growth, at the age of twenty-six, the heroic figure flashes a violent farewell to youth and young manhood. There is a struggle, a passionate wavering, a tremendous resistance, a complete triumph. And Martha knew the whole story!

It was this knowledge that fell about her like a mantle copied from an eternal model. Under its protection was peace, confidence, tenderness and truth. Sally had excited George, Martha *possessed* him!

Doubt, jealousy, fear were utterly unthinkable in the love of such a man. So they could go visiting back and forth in friendly warmth, frankness and freedom. She could even write letters dictated by George—to Sally. George was a giant in the field, a giant in the state, a giant in domestic love. To him Martha was ever "Dearest," or "Dearest Patsy."

And now the 1926 biographers would seize upon the evidence of his greatness, dip it in the acid of lechery, and shrink it to a whisper. Yes, we shall examine the letter in full.

CHAPTER IV

THE SALLY FAIRFAX SCANDAL

ONE of the 1926 biographers, in a sad but sane moment, slips away from sex and writes this:

"Late in 1777 the British Publicity Department brought out its masterpiece of propaganda . . . a volume made up of letters supposed to have been written by Washington . . . most of which were addressed to his wife or to his brothers."

It is intended that these letters shall produce a profound impression upon the populace. Washington is presented as a sorry figure. He is confessing that the war is a terrible blunder. Deploring his part in the mistake, he wishes he were well out of it. British rule is, after all, to be preferred to the rule of the mob. According to the British Intelligence Office these devastating documents expressing deep and remorseful sentiments were found on the person of Billy Lee, Washington's body-servant. The unfortunate Billy, being too sick to be moved in the army's wild retreat across New Jersey, was captured. Who could believe that a little packet of letters might be more powerful than 50,000 infantry?

All the superficial marks of genuineness are easily recognizable. Even "Dearest Patsy," Martha's loving nickname, stands out like snow on Monadnock.

But Billy Lee had not been sick; had not been captured; had never carried a packet of Washington's letters. The British were unable to produce a solitary specimen of Washington's handwriting. Washington himself, because of the obvious familiarity of the author with Martha and Mt. Vernon, believed the spurious epistles to be the work of John Randolph, a Tory refugee who at an earlier period had been a guest at Mt. Vernon but was now fled to England.

In the face of these wretched letters, the genuineness of which was accepted by thousands until their true character and purpose were revealed, it is incredible that two volumes should be written in 1926 with no more to vouch for them than a yellow newspaper clipping of 1877.

How easily one may romance with high-lights and shadows. Fiction is born to order. Spontaneous fiction is not born at all. It just appears. Behold a specimen.

John Randolph knew Sally Fairfax. He was an eyewitness of the friendship existing between her husband and the commander-in-chief of the Continental Army. He was familiar with Washington's

THE SALLY FAIRFAX SCANDAL

domestic life. He had never seen such a calmly happy pair. That Washington (1777) had been a devoted husband for nearly twenty years, during fifteen of which he had left his plantations at Mt. Vernon, unaccompanied by Martha, on but two brief occasions, was known to everybody in Virginia.

But Randolph knew more than this. He knew that Washington was saddled with all the responsibilities of the Revolution; that he was sorely handicapped by a sluggish Congress and a public spirit almost moribund. He knew that nothing could so step-up the distress of his mind as a shaft aimed at the heart of Martha. At least one of the letters would have to be free from coarseness and grossness because Martha was one woman who knew there was nothing coarse or gross in her husband's nature. To have brutally overdone the letter would have been fatal to its designs. It had to be subtle. It had to insinuate a secret affection for another. It had to exhibit a cruel and wholly unnatural slight to herself. How easy to conclude that the letter not published until 1877 was part of the 1777 propaganda. Of course there is no proof, but we are not for the moment dealing with proof. The mere complexion of plausibility is sufficient to the needs of the romancer. Cases come or go at any idler's bidding, but no case can be made gross at will. Whatever was gross or carnal in Washington's ani-

GREATEST OF MEN—WASHINGTON

mal nature was under harness. Even at that early age he had conquered self. Never was simple truth more apparent; more eloquently attested.

Strain, tug, italicize and construe as we will, to hammer out a case against Washington, we might at least remember the injunction "Let him who is without sin cast the first stone," and then read the letter. Here it is, written in the twenty-sixth year of Washington's life.

"CAMP AT FORT CUMBERLAND,
12th September, 1758.

"DEAR MADAM,

"Yesterday I was honored with your short but very agreeable favor of the first inst. How joyfully I catch at the happy occasion of renewing a correspondence which I feared was disrelished on your part, I leave to time, that never failing expositor of all things, and to a monitor equally faithful in my own breast, to testify. In silence I now express my joy; silence, which in some cases, I wish the present, speaks more intelligently than the sweetest eloquence.

"If you allow that any honor can be derived from my opposition to our present system of management, you destroy the merit of it entirely in me by attributing my anxiety to the animating prospect of possessing Mrs. Custis, when—I need not tell you, guess yourself. Should not my own Honor and country's welfare be the excitement?

" 'Tis true, I profess myself a votary of love. I

THE SALLY FAIRFAX SCANDAL

acknowledge that a lady is in the case, and further I confess that this lady is known to you. Yes, Madame, as well as she is to one who is too sensible of her charms to deny the Power whose influence he feels and must ever submit to. I feel the force of her amiable beauties in the recollection of a thousand tender passages that I could wish to obliterate, till I am bid to revive them. But experience, alas! sadly reminds me how impossible this is, and evinces an opinion which I have long entertained, that there is a Destiny which has the control of our actions, not to be resisted by the strongest efforts of Human Nature.

"You have drawn me, dear Madame, or rather I have drawn myself, into an honest confession of a simple Fact. Misconstrue not my meaning; doubt it not, nor expose it. The world has no business to know the object of my love, declared in this manner to you, when I want to conceal it. One thing above all things in this world I wish to know, and only one person of your acquaintance can solve me that, or guess my meaning. But adieu to this till happier times, if I ever shall see them. The hours at present are melancholy dull. Neither the rugged toils of war, nor the gentler conflict of A— B—s (Assembly Balls?), is in my choice. I dare believe you are as happy as you say. I wish I was happy also. Mirth, good humor, ease of mind, and—what else? —cannot fail to render you so and consummate your wishes.

"If one agreeable lady could almost wish herself a fine gentleman for the sake of another, I apprehend that many fine gentlemen will wish themselves finer e'er Mrs. Spotswood is possest. She has already become a reigning toast in this camp, and many there are in it who intend (fortune favoring) to make honorable scars speak the fullness of their merit, and be a messenger of their Love to Her.

"I cannot easily forgive the unseasonable haste of my last express, if he deprived me thereby of a single word you intended to add. The time of the present messenger is, as the last might have been, entirely at your disposal. I can't expect to hear from my friends more than this once before the fate of the expedition will some how or other be determined. I therefore beg to know when you set out for Hampton, and when you expect to return to Belvoir again. And I should be glad also to hear of your speedy departure, as I shall thereby hope for your return before I get down. The disappointment of seeing your family would give me much concern. From any thing I can yet see 'tis hardly possible to say when we shall finish. I don't think there is a probability of it till the middle of November. Your letter to Captain Gist I forwarded by a safe hand the moment it came to me. His answer shall be carefully transmitted.

"Col. Mercer, to whom I delivered your message and compliments, joins me very heartily in wishing you and the Ladies of Belvoir the perfect enjoyment of every happiness this world affords. Be assured that I am, dear Madame, with the most unfeigned regard, your most obedient and most obliged humble servant.

THE SALLY FAIRFAX SCANDAL

"N. B. Many accidents happening (to use a vulgar saying) between the cup and the lip, I choose to make the exchange of carpets myself, since I find you will not do me the honor to accept mine."

Assuming the genuineness of this letter, it justifies any number of contradictory interpretations, all but one of which do credit to the youthful Washington. The exception must appeal to italics, must be squeezed and strained to give it point. Its shadowy history would keep it out of any court. Its still more shadowy meaning destroys its value as an illuminating human document. Innocent on all counts but one, and scarcely doubtful on that, it reveals nothing, yet is the inspiration of two volumes.

Washington is far from happy as he writes. He wants Martha and her delicate children, but will be at camp or in the field he knows not how long.

Sally knows Martha and suspects an engagement. He wishes she might approve, for she and her husband are to be Martha's neighbors and he hopes they will be her friends.

He has always detested gossip and it will be time enough to let the world know of the affair of his heart when his country's troubles shall have been composed.

He may die in action. Martha's wound will be all the deeper because of her recollection of those

GREATEST OF MEN—WASHINGTON

thousand tender passages. If they had only been postponed!

And then the haunting doubt! Does Martha really love him? She is the only person of Sally's acquaintance who can answer that. At any rate he hopes Sally is happy.

He drops the melancholy mood and turns to the life of the camp, Mrs. Spotswood and the stir she has made. Secrecy? Captain Gist, Colonel Mercer and the ladies of Belvoir constitute strange secrets. Where there are so many custodians of secrecy there are no secrets to custode.

And what an anti-climax to such "sublime passion!" The gorgeous episode, "redeeming Washington to humanity," ends abruptly in an *exchange of carpets*.

CHAPTER V

AN ASTOUNDING PUZZLE

THE 1926 biographers admit that not the least astounding puzzle in the Sally Fairfax letter was Washington's motive for writing it at all, but conclude that however confusing to his idolaters, the letter itself "redeems Washington to humanity" and, however pitiful as a confession, it is "magnificent as passion." One of them says that the suppression, editing and destruction of such letters have led people to describe Washington as a silent man, a cold man, a man under almost perfect self-control.

No trait is more manifest in the character of any man than Washington's almost perfect self-control, nor is anything more clearly established than his lack of coldness. Above all things he was not a silent man. No other figure of history has given the world so many volumes of self-expression. Yet in the American government's vast wealth of Washington manuscripts not one objectionable phrase has ever been found. Tremendous stress is laid upon the Jared Sparks suppressions and editings. J. C. Fitzpatrick, assistant chief of the Manuscript Division of the Library of Con-

GREATEST OF MEN—WASHINGTON

gress who has charge of all the Washington letters and account books possessed by the government, and who made available everything connected with Washington to the 1926 biographers, informs me that Jared Sparks rendered a disservice to Washington, whose letters never did need, and need not now, any rhetorical tinkering. Moreover the unprinted and unprintable accusations against Washington now going their pornographic rounds among prominent newspapermen are wholly groundless—clumsy and insupportable fictions oozing from decadent minds, with not a solitary fact or fragment of fact to justify them.

Alexander J. Wall, librarian of the New York Historical Society, who has charge of more than a hundred Washington letters, is happiest when showing them to students as evidence of their author's loftiness of spirit and cleanness of speech.

I have been personally informed by a friend of the 1926 biographers, an associate of one of them, that Washington's philanderings in New York during the Revolution were notorious. The statement was made in the home and in the presence of a newspaper publisher, and within a week was repeated to me as historical fact by an official of a prominent publishing house.

When did these philanderings occur? During the Revolution, of course, when Washington was

AN ASTOUNDING PUZZLE

away from Mt. Vernon for a period of eight years and eight months. Examine their historicity. They are set forth in the General's own Account of Expenses, while Commander-in-Chief of the Continental Army, 1775-1783. This account shows that his wife shared 42 months of hardship with him, in camp, among the soldiers, under privations and distress, such as no other American army from that day to this has had to endure. What kind of a woman was she to face such an ordeal? What kind of man was he to inspire any woman to prefer suffering with him rather than comfort and luxury without him?

From the moment the army went into winter quarters, annually throughout the war, Martha joined her husband and did not leave him until the army took the field for action. She was with him everywhere except under gun-fire. Read this entry in Washington's own hand, July 1, 1783:

"To Mrs. Washington's Travellg Expenses in coming to & returning from my Winter Qrs. annually pr acct—The money to defray which being taken from my private purse & brot with her from Virginia."

"On acct of Mrs. Washington's expenses from Virga to my Winter Quarters & back again to Virginia according to the mem ms & accts wch I have rec ~~from her~~ those who accompanied her

GREATEST OF MEN—WASHINGTON

		Lawful		
1775 Dec	To amount of her Expences from Virginia to Cambridge	85	2	6
1776 July	To Ditto from New York to Virginia after the Enemy Landed on Staten Ild Including her residence at Phila at Board for sometime Acct	180	2	8
1777 Mar.	To Ditto from Virginia to Morris Town while the Troops lay in Winter Qts there	61	10	
May	To Ditto from Morristown to Virginia including a few days stay in Phila	74	—	
1778 Feb	To Ditto from Virginia to Valley Forge	52	8	6
June	To Ditto from Valley Forge back to Virga from that place when the army took ye Fd	54		
Dec ?	To Ditto to Philad where I then was at the request of Congress	48	—	
1779 June	To Ditto back to Virginia from Middle Brook when the Army marched from its Cantonment at that place	72	—	
Dec ?	To Ditto in coming to Morristown when the Army was Quartered in the Vicinity of it	63	5	
June 1780	To Ditto on her Return to Virg from that place	68	—	
Nov ?	To Ditto her Expe to My Qrs at New Windsor	78	6	8
June 1781	To Ditto back to Virginia from thence, when the Army took the Field includg a few days stay in Phila	85	—	

AN ASTOUNDING PUZZLE

July 1782	To her Expenses from Newburgh to Virginia	72		
Dec ?	To Ditto from Virginia to Newburgh	70	5	8
		1064	1	0

E Excepted
G Washington

July 1st 1783

As soon as the hazards of the summer campaigns were brought to an end it was Washington's custom to dispatch an aide-de-camp to Mt. Vernon as Martha's personal escort to Cambridge, Morristown, Valley Forge, Middle Brook, New Windsor, Newburgh, or wherever the army might be. When the road lay dangerously near the enemy's line a military escort accompanied her. When she was absent from Mt. Vernon, Lund Washington took charge under the following written orders from the General addressed to him from Cambridge:

"Let the hospitality of the house, with respect to the poor, be kept up. Let no one go away hungry. If any of this kind of people should be in want of corn, supply their necessities, provided it does not encourage them in idleness; and I have no objection to your giving my money in charity to the amount of forty or fifty pounds a year, when you think it well bestowed."

This from the philanderer, the man described by Gladstone as "the purest figure in history."

CHAPTER VI

FOUR PHILANDERING EPISTLES

PERHAPS there has been mistake somewhere. If Martha Washington's presence at the General's quarters throughout the Revolution means anything it means the necessity of shifting the time and scenes of her husband's philanderings to another period. Very well. We go back to an earlier date. We are again at Mt. Vernon. The House of Burgesses holds its sessions at Williamsburg, 160 miles from the Washington homestead. Washington attends these sessions in the spring and fall. Mrs. Washington accompanies him. She rides in his coach; he on horse-back beside her.

During the fifteen years following his marriage these official visits to Williamsburg, except for two other absences from home, are all the calumniators have to work upon. In 1770 he did push through the wilderness to the Ohio to look after the bounty lands which he and his companions in arms had received from the government for their military services during the campaigns against the French and Indians. He was accompanied by his friend and neighbor, Dr. Craik, and three servants on horse-

FOUR PHILANDERING EPISTLES

back, and was gone nine weeks and one day, longer than he had been away from Mt. Vernon at any time between 1759 and 1775. The other departure is found in his visit to New York City in May, 1773, accompanied by young Jack Custis, Martha's son, whom he brought up to New York for the purpose of entering him in King's College. The journey northward with the boy consumed sixteen days. Unencumbered, he hurried home, making the return trip in nine days. Philandering in the wilderness! A new occupation for homo sapiens! Philandering on a hurried ride through a thinly populated country-side! Another new occupation!

The roads were "infamous." Why was he so eager to get back home? Because his heart was there. Easily understood are his letters at the beginning of the war. He is Virginia's delegate in the Congress. The Assembly presses him unanimously to accept the command of the colonial forces. So he writes his "Dear Patsy"—his Martha—mother of "the Sweet, Innocent Girl" who died shortly after her brother Jacky had been fixed at College:

"My Dearest:—I am now set down to write to you on a subject, which fills me with inexpressible concern, and this concern is greatly aggravated and increased, when I reflect upon the uneasiness I know it will give you. It has been determined in Congress, that the whole army raised for the defence of the American cause shall be put under my care, and that it is necessary for me to proceed immediately to Boston to take upon me the command of it.

"You may believe me, my dear Patsy, when I assure you, in the most solemn manner, that, so far from seeking this appointment, I have used every endeavor in my power to avoid it, not only from my unwillingness to part with you and the family, but from a consciousness of its being a trust too great for my capacity, and that I should enjoy more real happiness in one month with you at home, than I have the most distant prospect of finding abroad, if my stay were to be seven times seven years. But as it has been a kind of destiny, that has thrown me upon this service, I shall hope that my undertaking it is designed to answer some good purpose. You might, and I suppose did perceive, from the tenor of my letters, that I was apprehensive I could not avoid this appointment, as I did not pretend to intimate when I should return. That was the case. It was utterly out of my power to refuse this appointment, without exposing my character to such censures, as would have reflected dishonor upon myself, and given pain to my friends. This, I am sure, could not, and ought not, to be pleasing to you, and must have lessened me considerably in my own esteem.

"I shall rely, therefore, confidently on that Providence, which has heretofore preserved and been bountiful to me, not doubting but that I shall return safe to you in the fall. I shall feel no pain from the toil or the danger of the campaign; my unhappiness will flow from the uneasiness I know you will feel from being left alone. I therefore beg, that you will summon your whole fortitude, and pass your time as agreeably as possible. Nothing will give me so much sincere satisfaction as to hear this, and to hear it from your own pen. My earnest and ardent desire is, that you would pursue any plan that is most likely to produce content, and a tolerable degree of tranquillity; as it must add greatly to my uneasy feelings to hear, that you are dissatisfied or complaining at what I really could not avoid.

"As life is always uncertain, and common prudence dictates to every man the necessity of settling his temporal concerns, while it is in his power, and while the mind is calm and undisturbed, I have, since I came to this place (for I had not time to do it before I left home) got Colonel Pendleton to draft a will for me, by the directions I gave him, which will I now enclose. The provisions made for you in case of my death will, I hope, be agreeable.

"I shall add nothing more, as I have several letters to write, but to desire that you will remember me to your friends, and to assure you that I am, with the most unfeigned regard, my dear Patsy, your affectionate &c."

Then this letter to young Jack Custis, "Patsy's" son:

"My great concern is the thought of leaving your mother under the uneasiness which I fear this affair will throw her into; I therefore hope, expect, and

GREATEST OF MEN—WASHINGTON

indeed have no doubt, of your using every means in your power to keep up her spirits, by doing everything to promote her quiet. At any time I hope it is unnecessary for me to say that I am always pleased with yours and Nellie's abidance at Mt. Vernon; much less upon this occasion, when I think it absolutely necessary for the peace and satisfaction of your mother; a consideration which I have no doubt will have due weight with you, and require no argument to enforce."

To his brother, John Augustine, he writes:

"How far I shall succeed is another point, but this I am sure of, that, in the worst event, I shall have the consolation of knowing if I act to the best of my judgment that the blame ought to lodge upon the appointers, not the appointed, as it was by no means a thing of my seeking, or proceeding from any hint of my friends. I shall hope that my friends will visit and endeavor to keep up the spirits of my wife, as much as they can, as my departure will, I know, be a cutting stroke upon her; and on this account alone I have many very disagreeable sensations. I hope you and my sister, although the distance is great, will find as much leisure this summer as to spend a little time at Mt. Vernon."

Washington knew Mt. Vernon would be desolate. His deep solicitude was for Martha. He did not know that he would not see Mt. Vernon again, except for a momentary and accidental visit in 1781,

FOUR PHILANDERING EPISTLES

on his march to Yorktown, for eight years and eight months.

He was forty-three years old when the war began; nearly fifty-two when it ended. He was twenty-six when he married. From that time to his death-bed in 1799 all the evidence conclusively establishes not only his innocence of philandering but his abhorrence of it. The romancers deliberately close their eyes to the life of this man to whom honor and fidelity were greater passions than any sting the flesh can ever feel.

His rebuke of Lund Washington, who, to save the burning of Mt. Vernon, with neither arms nor men to defend it, was guilty of an act that Washington had best himself describe, is a classic of honor:

"I am sorry to hear of your loss. I am a little sorry to hear of my own; but that which gives me most concern is, that you should go and board the enemy's vessels and furnish them with refreshments. It would have been a less painful circumstance to me to have heard, that in consequence of your non-compliance with their request they had burnt my House, and laid the Plantation in ruins. You ought to have considered yourself as my representative, and should have reflected on the bad example of communicating with the enemy, and making a voluntary offer of refreshments to them, with a view to prevent a conflagration. It was not in your power,

GREATEST OF MEN—WASHINGTON

I acknowledge, to prevent them from sending a flag on shore, and you did right to meet it; but you should, in the same instant that the business of it was unfolded, have declared explicitly, that it was improper for you to yield to the request; after which, if they had proceeded to help themselves by force, you could have but submitted; and, being unprovided for defense, this was to be preferred to a feeble opposition, which only serves as a pretext to burn and destroy."

Can we name a philanderer capable of writing such a letter under such circumstances? Honor cannot be at white heat at one end, sodden at the other.

Can Martha enlighten us now? Most wonderfully. Five months have passed. Washington is writing his brother John Augustine, October 13, 1775, from the camp at Cambridge. Within musket-shot of each other he has finished his lines of defense against the enemy. He submits to a daily cannonade without returning a shot, from scarcity of powder. He realizes that the affair will be long drawn out and that he will be unable to return to his family. He knows that Martha's journey to him will be beset with difficulties, yet he longs for her. Will she come? So he writes his brother:

"I have laid before her a state of the difficulties which must attend the journey and left it to her

FOUR PHILANDERING EPISTLES

own choice. My love to my sister and the little ones is sincerely tendered, and I am, with true regard, your most affectionate brother."

Will Martha come to him? Henceforth the comforts and safety of Mt. Vernon mean nothing to her. She will be with him to the end. She will make the dreadful journey every year for eight years, regardless of the location of his winter quarters, and will not leave him until he again takes the field. He had left it to her own choice, and she had chosen. Love could find the way. Has it ever occurred to the modern critic that Martha, the woman, was worthy of a pure love? that she was the custodian of a pure love? that she could make all the more sacred the pure love of a mere man? Martha, the wife and mother, was Washington's other self. Her devotion to him was a reaction, a recognition, a response. The two were one. The one was a holy union.

The pure integrity of his heart was like that of his mind. In the last line of page 35 you observed an instance of his reverence of truth, even in trifles. Not Martha herself, but rather her escort, furnished the expense account. Washington at once corrected the slip of the pen, drawing a line through the words "from her."

CHAPTER VII

STUPIDITY! CRUELTY!! SLAVES!!!

WHAT are we to expect from a Washington biographer who attempts to show that Washington must have been a philanderer because even the clergy of his time were rotten? Page 20, "the clergy are given to evil living. They are a laughing stock or objects of disgust. They are obscene, addicted to the race field, the card table, the ballroom, the theatre—nay, more, to the drunken revel." The same biographer, page 310, forgetting his own page 20, emits the following: "In his despair Washington thought that a chaplain might have a good influence on his cowardly brigands."

Washington's heart is sick. More and more innocent people are being killed by reason of the dissolute and conscienceless character of the handful of men at his command. It is the year 1756, twenty years before the Revolution. The tears of women are moving him

"into such deadly sorrow that I solemnly declare, if I know my own mind, I could offer myself a willing sacrifice to the butchering enemy, provided that would contribute to the people's ease. I am dis-

STUPIDITY! CRUELTY!! SLAVES!!!

tracted what to do. Three families were murdered the night before last, at the distance of less than twelve miles from this place. There are now no militia in this country. When there were they could not be brought to action."

Indian atrocities are multiplying. His men are deserting. His helplessness is complete. He sees that nothing short of the death penalty will save the defenseless creatures whom he has been sent by Governor Dinwiddie to protect.

In his anguish, because the clergy are "so rotten," he begs for a chaplain in order to exert "a good influence on his men." How stupid he is to expect help from a chaplain! How he despises some common people and loves others! Yet knowing the clergy are evil, he seeks good in them. This is inspiration! The biographers, the inspired!!

Here we have best-selling biography and a conclusion: Washington, bleeding for his people,

"was to the last an aristocrat of the slightest possible interest in the common people, who grew up to regard the common run, as he called them, with a profound contempt that made it impossible for him to act upon or even to understand the theory that all men are created free and equal."

Of course a man abominating the common run was cruel to his slaves. Why not? It was the custom. One of the biographers makes a point of

GREATEST OF MEN—WASHINGTON

stating that burning alive was a legal punishment for negro slaves convicted of insurrection against their masters. So it was. But what's the point? How is it aimed at Washington? When did Washington burn a slave?

Every man knows where the "slave-cruelty" stories came from. Washington court-martialled Major-Gen. Charles Lee, who, in command of the advance guard, ordered the American troops to retreat at Monmouth, New Jersey. Lee never forgave the General, and in his bitterness never thought of charging Washington with philandering, but did charge him with inhuman treatment of his slaves.

What about Washington's letter of 1786 to Robert Morris?

"There is not a man living who wishes more sincerely than I do to see a plan adopted for the abolition of slavery. But there is only one proper and effectual mode by which it can be accomplished, and that is by legislative authority; and this, as far as my suffrage will go, shall never be wanting."

What did he mean when he wrote John F. Mercer, of Virginia, 1786?

"I never mean, unless some particular circumstance should compel me to it, to possess another slave by purchase, it being among my first wishes to see some plan adopted by which slavery in this country may be abolished by law."

STUPIDITY! CRUELTY!! SLAVES!!!

Even Abraham Lincoln found it not easy, with public sentiment to support him, to give expression to such Anti-Slavery views. In Washington's day there was no sentiment but his own against slavery. In this he stood out against the mass a solitary figure, "despising the common run."

What did he mean when he wrote to Robert Willis, his nephew, 1799, four months before his death?

"I have more negroes on my estate than can be employed to any advantage in the farming system: and I shall never turn planter thereon. To sell the overplus I cannot, because I am principalled against that kind of traffic in the human species. To hire them out is almost as bad, because they cannot be disposed of in families as I have an aversion to that system."

No wonder Thomas Jefferson could write of him:

"His integrity was most pure; his justice the most inflexible I have ever known; no motives of interest or consanguinity of friendship or hatred, being able to bias his decision. He was indeed a wise, a good, and a great man."

In 1927, at Mt. Vernon, I had the privilege of talking with the very last of the descendants of the old Washington slaves, George Ford, 71 years of

GREATEST OF MEN—WASHINGTON

age, once owned by John Augustine Washington, Jr. He was born in the old kitchen and is still employed on the ground as a Mt. Vernon police. His father, West Ford, was owned by John Augustine, and he, too, was born at Mt. Vernon. George Ford's grandfather was owned by Judge Bushrod Washington, son of George Washington's brother, and inheritor of the Washington home. Ford's grandfather, who knew Washington, told him he was never cruel to his slaves but that some of his overseers, some of them black men too, were guilty of cruelty, but never of a kind that could possibly get to the ears of the General.

The provisions of his will affecting the freedom of his slaves and their comfort were not inspired by cruelty. A pen capable of insinuating that he had no affection for his mother, in the light of the evidence to the contrary, is capable of any poison, including the malignant, "bundling" paragraphs, which, in keeping with the rest of the anti-Washington virus, the biographer does not even attempt to connect with Washington's name, though in an off moment, page 165, he says: "He seems to have treated his slaves very well." It's all biography, you know; modernistic, sequential, ultra-new, provided only that we scrutinize not too closely the muddled state we find it in.

CHAPTER VIII

IDEALIST OR TURNIP-SOWER

NOW we have the man, Washington, settled down on his plantations, at the age of twenty-eight, in the year 1760, and the first thing we learn from his own pen New Year's Day is filled with significance. Mr. Daniel French has engaged to let him have some pork at 20*s*. Because the price is risen to 22s. 6d. Mr. French repudiates the contract. Washington does not abuse the man. He refers to the episode merely as "an instance of Mr. French's great love of money."

We should have a mawkish essay on the dastardliness of breached contracts and a slew of bitter invectives denouncing the knave for his dishonesty. What happens? Washington pays the extra price and never again mentions the matter. He is too busy hauling the seine for fish. He hasn't yet got his livestock in shape. He must buy corn and a keg of butter. He doesn't think he is the greatest farmer in the world and never intimates that the flesh of his own animals is the best ever. He kills and dresses "751 pounds Hogs and other weight of

GREATEST OF MEN—WASHINGTON

Beeves that Jack brought down, two of which were *tolerable good*."

Most of the time he is in the saddle, except when he rides in his "chariot" with the family to church. Saturday evening, January 5th, because of the great cold and the high wind he sends Mrs. Fairfax home in the chariot, which fails to return in time to enable the Washingtons to get to church. So prevented he records the fact, as if it really matters.

According to the caricature Washington had no religion. Nevertheless his diary contains 124 references to the effort he makes to get to public worship at a time when public worship is possible only to those who are ready to put themselves out through bad roads, long distances and uncomfortable rides. The mud is deep! The ruts are deeper! Yet we have 124 round trips for certain—twenty miles of jolting coach—at least four hours of sacrifice with services between.

February 15, 1760, he

"Went to a Ball at Alexandria, where Musick and dancing was the chief Entertainment . . . in a convenient Room detached for the purpose abounded great plenty of Bread and Butter, some Biscuits with Tea, and Coffee which the Drinkers of coud not Distinguish from Hot water sweetened. Be it remembered that pockethandkerchiefs servd the

IDEALIST OR TURNIP-SOWER

purposes of Table Cloths and Napkins and that no Apologies were made for either."

Obviously eating was not the "Chief Entertainment." The young Washington actually admires the unaffected simplicity of this "Bread and Butter Ball." It is all very amusing but does not excite ridicule or contempt.

At this time he is sending ewes and lambs to the mill to be fatted. He is grinding his own wheat (47 bushels) and bottling 91 dozen cider. Riding out to his plantations he is astonished to find his carpenter, Richard Stephens, *hard at work with an axe*.

"Very extraordinary this," he says, February 2d. Again February 4th he notices that Stephens really is at work. A third time he catches the indolent fellow engaged in honest labor when apparently nobody is looking and the spectacle pleases him so greatly he has to make note of it.

George, Tom, Mike and young Billy are hewing but 120 feet in the day. They are able to do 180 feet of plank. Where is the horsewhip? They ought to be driven in keeping with the character of the driver. But the driver merely notes that because of the difference between the working of Poplar and the working of other wood there may be some excuse for the low output "which some *future* observations must make known." Surely this is not rashness, not violence, not inhuman cruelty. On the contrary the suggestion of patience and quiet amusement is more than hint. It is reality!

March 21, 1760, the frivolous flirt and inconstant husband begins the grafting of forty cherry trees, twelve Bullock Hearts—a large black May Cherry, eighteen very fine early May Cherries, and ten Carnation Cherries.

In rapid succession he sets out "55 cuttings of the Madeira grape where the plums are," and is grafting and planting "pretty little early June pears at the end of the quinces, and Spanish pears, a very valuable Fruit, and butter pears esteemed among the finest, and black pears, a large course fruit for baking."

He finishes the month in grafting winter boon cherries, summer boon cherries, Bergamy pears, New Town Pippins and Maryland Red Strick apples. The following month he is sowing barley near the tobacco house, hauling the seine for herring and white fish.

In April and May he is grinding corn; mixing his composts for fertilizer; planting wheat, oats and barley; drawing bricks; burning lime; sending up hides to be tanned. He buys a pipe of wine which Captain McKee brought from Madeira, a chest of lemons, and some other trifles. His life is utterly full.

IDEALIST OR TURNIP-SOWER

With sheep-shearing, field-grubbing, timber-cutting, fence-building, horse-doctoring, candle-making, hog-butchering, lard-rendering, tar-melting and much entertaining of visitors, most of whom stay overnight and depart in the morning after breakfast, we leave him until July 31, 1761.

Here we find the man who later in his life, if he will only keep the peace and be as one of the other Tories, can have any gift of his own naming from the Crown. What is he doing? Sowing turnips.

Yes, this make-believe patriot who really does resist the blandishments of the British government, who really does place his wealth and comfort in jeopardy, who really does put his head in the noose with everything to lose, nothing to gain, except for the benefit of his fellows, is sowing turnips.

CHAPTER IX

HARD DRINK AND GAMBLING

IN 1763, at his plantations in King William, at Bridge Quarter, and at Ship Landing, Washington has thirty-five Negro sharers and overseers, 227 head of cattle including work-steers, almost as many sheep and lamb, 200 head of sows for breeding, porkers and young pigs, and nearly 200,000 each of corn holes and tobacco hills. He is thirty-one years old and his farms are growing. The hard drinker's neglect of the industry of his estate is spectacular. He is cutting and stacking sixty acres of wheat, more than fifty acres of rye at River and Creek Quarters, Muddy Hole Farm and Dogue Run Farm.

Throughout July and August he makes hay of timothy and clover, plants roots in the peach and apple orchard, sows wheat and spelts. In September his corn is beginning to show and he is ready for barley, rye and English walnuts.

The frost bites his tobacco and his fodder. There is no lament. The man who notes that a little negro child looks pinched and wan and *brings her down to the house* for Martha to physic, instead of sending somebody out with a dose of impersonal

HARD DRINK AND GAMBLING

medicine, has little heart of course, and might be expected to thunder in the index when the frost defeats so much of his labor. But whatever else Washington might have been he was no thunderer, and it is quite obvious, though we haven't gone very far with him, for he is still very youngish, that the frivolous flirt has been grotesquely maligned.

In March, 1764, the clay idol is grafting more cherries, plums and pears. In August he is trimming tobacco, gathering peaches in barrels, making ready to plow his turnips. Later he transplants Lucerne below the garden and sows rows of St. Foine.

The press at his cider mill is creaking. His spelts and oats are going into the ground. He is curing and stacking hay and laying in fodder for the winter. The Devil's Workshop is "To Let."

In March, 1765, the unstable, unfaithful and physically-tainted swiller of rum is grafting English mulberries on wild mulberry stalks on the side of the hill near the spring path. The stalks are very milky. The experiment is designed to discover a new hardihood, a new vitality. The man who squanders his time at cards probes deeply into Nature and strives with all his might to produce a new Gloucester White.

All his livestock are branded "G.W." and he is beginning to develop a reputation as the best miller of flour in the Colonies, a reputation that makes the inspectors at the ports of entry pass any flour bearing the legend "G.W." without looking at it. They know it to be all that it ought to be. Uninterrupted constancy of experience has taught them and they refuse to frivol their time in examinations that reveal only perfection. Scandal and "G.W." are incompatibles.

Between chores Washington indulges much in fox-hunting. When he chases an animal four hours and *fails* to get it by reason of its superior craft and its ability to enter holes where neither dog nor man may follow he records the event. Hence when he captures two foxes in a single afternoon we find no sane excuse for disputing the truth of his assertion.

From his bulls, cows, yearlings, calves, sheep, ewes and hogs he turns to sawing palings for a goose-yard, and then to his hounds. In February, 1768, while clearing more land of its timber at Point of Woods, he lets us know that his dogs at this time are Tartar, Jupiter, Trueman, Truelove, June, Duchess, Lady, Forester, Sancho, Ringwood, Sentwell, Chanter, Singer and Busy. Chivalrous names for dogs!

Two of his hounds, as if in a musing hour his mood had penetrated the future, even unto the generation of his defamers, are named Tipler and Drunkard. Merry mischief, this.

HARD DRINK AND GAMBLING

Now we find a choice morsel to chew over. It is January 16, 1768. Washington is thirty-six years old. His profligacy is beginning at last to show itself, like his old corn mill which has gone to ruin, the timbers of it having rotted. He is off his guard. Mr. Charles Dick, a merchant of Fredericksburg, Mr. George Muse of Caroline County, and Washington's own brother Charles, are with him. The day before they had been shooting together.

Now comes the disclosure. In a brazen, unshamed hour Washington writes: "At home all day at Cards —it's snowing."

Thanks to John C. Fitzpatrick, we learn that the entries for gains and losses at cards and other play are as carefully entered in Washington's accounts as all other income and expenditures. There is an entry January, 1765: "By Cash set aside for Card money £5."

Grouped throughout the years from 1772 to 1775 for cash won and lost at home, Fredericksburg, Williamsburg, Annapolis, and other places, the entries show a total loss at play of £6 3s. 3d. in four years, an average of 61 cents a month, *15 cents a week*. Obviously in addition to all his other defects Washington was a "piker." This characterization should be included among the rest. It lacks dignity and therefore is apt.

Now with a deep breath we may go out with him

for mallards and bald-face ducks, and when the snow clears we shall have to help him build a road from Mt. Vernon by the lane to Mr. Manley's, for in this at least he resembles Cæsar—he builds roads. Unlike Cæser he shoots sprigtails, teals and pheasants, and dallies with a hook and line. Isaak Walton, still frying on one side for his piscatorial dissipations, may moan: "Turn over, brother George. It's hotter over here!"

CHAPTER X

FOX-HUNTING AND DINNERS

IN 1769, in the month of April, in addition to sowing and threshing, Washington is hauling in whitefish and herring in great numbers. When not in the saddle he is attending sessions of the Burgesses or dining with gentlemen. The odd thing about his companions is that so many of them are doctors and clergymen, and relations by blood or marriage.

Of course he is ever in constant fear that the intimacies of such companionships will eventually find him out. His hidden life is ever in danger of betraying itself. What a stupid lot these intimates must be never to suspect a truth so easily dug up a hundred and fifty years later by gentlemen with fountain pens.

To be sure we find Washington at Ayscough's Tavern in Williamsburg, at Ye Daphne Inn, or at the Raleigh Tavern. Martha knows about these visits for the reason that she has never been blind, and frequently accompanying him has eyes to see whither she is going and whereat she has arrived.

Put this down; Washington is not ashamed to. In good weather or bad he drives to public worship.

GREATEST OF MEN—WASHINGTON

He really does believe in the Established Church. It's "foreign" of course, being British. But it's not Roman. Yet he sets down that he attends the High Mass at a Catholic Church, and again Quaker services. He is not a religious man because he says so little about religion in his diary! He was never president at all because he says almost NOTHING about that high office in his diary!

It is Christmas eve, December 24, 1769. Washington "went to Prayers and spent the evening with Edward Jones," the overseer of his mother's plantation, at Julian's Tavern, Fredericksburg. Undutiful son!

Why does he make such a mockery of prayers and why is he so friendly with the overseer of his mother's plantation? There is something sinister back of this if only the biographers could come upon it. Alas, for the corruption of the human race, that such a dismal and unnatural circumstance should come to pass.

By February, 1770, Washington being thirty-eight years of age, his fisheries have become an important factor in the management of his many other affairs. February 3, after agreeing with Joseph Goart to raise stone out of the Washington quarry, he engages with Robert Adam to take all his fish up to 500 barrels, and more than this quantity if he can get casks to put them in. Washington pro-

FOX-HUNTING AND DINNERS

vides the fish house but not the salt. He is to receive £10 for the use of the house and 3s. a thousand in Virginia money for his herring. For the whitefish he is to receive 8s. 4d. in Maryland currency for each hundred.

He has built a new corn house, sowed and reaped his flax, has fished for sturgeon from breakfast to dinner, catching *none*, has gone ashooting and harehunting with the hounds, indifferently successful, and like a gladsome boy has bought a new rifle for £6 10d., whereafter nothing will satisfy him until he gives suitable entertainment to the dancing-master who teaches the young people of Fairfax. He has become a fencing master himself and reads books, as the extraordinary improvement in the style of his writing indicates.

He is a typical country gentleman who entertains sumptuously at breakast, dinner and supper; whose home is constantly filled with guests. Yet wherever there is *work to be done* either for himself or for the community at large he is at hand.

Wherever there are outside dinners, barbeques or balls he and Martha are present.

When he goes into Machodack Creek fishing he dines with the Reverend Mr. Smith, in all probability another hard-drinking, card-playing deceiver. He now has a Schooner which he built himself, but he remains faithful to fox-hunting.

GREATEST OF MEN—WASHINGTON

Seeing an innumerable quantity of wild turkeys or many deer watering and browsing, some of which he kills, he enters the fact. When he receives a quarter of very fine buffalo from Kiashute, one of the Six Nation Chiefs, he jots it down.

At Pittsburg, Thursday, November 22, 1770, he spends an enormous sum in entertaining Dr. John Connolly, a Loyalist, at Samples' Tavern, where the dinner costs him £26 1s. 10d. The mysterious purport of this expenditure can only be suspected in the light of what happened a few years later to all Loyalists. No man has fathomed the abysmal secret! Moreover Washington was visiting his "Bounty Lands."

So we find him extending his activities until at the Home House he has a val de chambre, Will; two waiters, Frank and Austin; two cooks, Hercules and Nathan; three drivers and stablers, Giles, Joe and Paris; three semstresses, Betty, Lame Alice and Charlotte; two housemaids, Sal and Caroline, with Doll and Jenny almost past service; two washers, Sal Brass and Dolly; four spinners, Alice, Myrtilla, Kitty and Winnie; one stock-keeper, Frank; an old jobber, Cook Jack; seven laborers, Gunner, Boatswain, Sam, Anthony, Tom Davis, Will and Joe; one wagoner, Jack; one carter, Sims; one gardener, Bristol; four carpenters, Isaac, James, Sambo and Tom Nokes; two blacksmiths, Nat and George; one

FOX-HUNTING AND DINNERS

knitter, Peter; one miller, Ben; three coopers, Jack, Tom and Davy.

There are sixty-seven children about the place, with 216 workers and overseers on the various plantations. After a little while we shall find them "teasing" their cruel master. Teasing is the word. It surely was the custom of abused slaves to "tease" the wielder of the lash!

CHAPTER XI

ALL OFF TO THE RACES

WASHINGTON, the adventurer and philanderer, is strangely interested in experiments with Siberian wheat. He is fanning heated corn, harrowing the ground for his Albany peas, dallying with carrots and potatoes, pulling in 300 shad at a draft, noting a method of preserving pumpkins by splitting them in two, taking out the inside, then turning the rind part up for three days to dry, after which, packed in straw, they are to keep well throughout the winter.

In his botanical garden he is experimenting with Illinois nuts, Gloucester hickory nuts, pistachio nuts and walnuts. He is improving the character of his milch cows and is producing enormous quantities of sweet butter and fine cheeses. He contracts for loads of good and clean shells to be ground for fertilizer and poultry food. When offered, short-weight and dirty, he rejects them. His carelessness knows no bounds. A hard-drinking profligate, a card shark and land speculator, a dancing popinjay might be expected to be careless. Let us see him at his worst.

ALL OFF TO THE RACES

He is shipping fifty barrels of flour at a time from his mill. He is making wool and cotton garments from his own shearings and fields. He sells fatted beeves and wethers to the butchers of Alexandria. He establishes his own paddock for deer and produces the venison served at his table. For the maintenance of the ditchers in his swamp, his lowest grade of labor, he provides a pound of salt meat or a pound and a half of fresh meat with eighteen ounces of brown bread, a pint of spirits and a bottle of milk every day, and insists that the bread shall be baked at his own house and that the meat shall be cooked by Morris's wife. In addition he pays the ditchers 12d. per rod for the ditches.

Your mere lover of sport would be expected occasionally to run short of corn for bread. Washington does just that. So he mixes middlings and ship-stuff for himself and his whites, and ship-stuff and rye, a still more nutritious bread, for his blacks.

He imports coffee and molasses from Dutch Guiana and leaves many evidences of a sweet tooth behind him. He also leaves evidences of a sweet temper. Riding through his plantations he discovers that "Most of my people have gone to the races. Ferry people all gone to the race and those at home idle. Overseer being gone to the race."

He does not rage. There is no stern rebuke. His people are human. They know their master is human. They do not hesitate, the whole ilk and boodle of them, *to go to the races*.

Is any man mad enough to believe that fear-crazed, whip-driven, savagely-punished slaves and their bulldozing overseers would dare take the liberty of laying down their work for a trip to the races?

The very fact that they did these things and that Washington mentions them with the same emotion induced by his cabbage, corn and tobacco should constitute proof for all time that he was a just master and a humane man. Should there still be doubt on the point the extraordinary provisions of his will with respect to his slaves should forever settle the issue.

But here he is bringing bullocks from the mill meadow to be stall-fed, building a new fishing boat, inventing a plow, cutting and stowing ice for the summer, storing 2,000 chestnuts in a box of sand to put out the following spring. The wretched man's conscience-stricken mind will not let him rest. He must conduct experiments to determine the difference in terms of economy between burning spermacetti and tallow candles, finding that the latter are better as thirty-two is to ten and a half.

Utterly ignoring the needs of poorer neighbors, he lays up at a single time 15,885 pounds of his own pork, which, he writes, is "for consumption at my

ALL OFF TO THE RACES

Table, the use of my People and *the Poor who are distressed for it.*"

How could son of woman be born with such unhappy sentiments in his heart?

Look at him pulling parsnips, distilling whiskey, prowling about for honey, decoying 50,000 herring in a single draft, burying buckwheat, laying in the cold ground the seeds of melons by the overseer's house. Craft and cruelty, nothing else!

Watch him as he counts 3114 Gentleman Pease, 2268 York River Pease, 1375 and 1330 other varieties, 1186 early Black Eye Pease, and 1473 Bunch Hominy Beans to the pint. Here indeed is delirium, frivolous folly, philandering complex. Why should he stoop to such petty and ridiculous occupation? Alas, he seeks to know the actual number of seeds that will plant a given acreage without wanton waste. He wants the farmers of his country to prosper. Monstrous man! The biographers of 1926 poke fun at him for this.

Look at him again at his worst. He worries over the illness of little Patcy Custis who died suddenly June 19, 1773. The following day he writes:

"Yesterday the Sweet Innocent Girl Entered into a more happy and peaceful abode than any she has met with in the afflicted Path she hitherto has trod. She rose from dinner about 4 o'clock in better health and spirits than she appeared to have been in for some time; soon after which she was seized with one of her usual Fits, and expired in it, in less than two minutes without uttering a word, a groan or scarce a sigh—This sudden and unexpected blow, I scarce need add has almost reduced my poor Wife to the lowest ebb of Misery."

Then follow many entries: "I continued at home all day." "I continued at home all day." "I continued at home all day." "I continued at home all day." The human heart knows why.

CHAPTER XII

BRAGGADOCIO AT ITS WORST

THE dull and prosy farmer writes shortly before the end to his dear Tobias Lear:

"Mrs. Washington & myself will do what I believe has not been done within the last twenty years by us,—that is set down to dinner by ourselves."

To use his own description of it, his house has become "a well-resorted tavern." Coach loads are discharged at his door. He longs for an old-fashioned day of quiet with Martha alone. Such a day is at last in sight—the first of its kind in twenty years. He and Martha are to be privileged to dine together without company. The precious hour will take them back to the days which were the happiest they ever knew. Let us go back with them.

On the surface the colony is at peace. It has much to complain of against the Crown but is not thinking of war. Washington himself is writing:

"I do not know that I can muster up one tittle of news to communicate. In short the occurrences of

GREATEST OF MEN—WASHINGTON

this part of the world are at present scarce worth reciting; for, we live in a state of peaceful tranquility ourselves, so we are at very little trouble to inquire the operations against the Cherokees, who are the only people that disturb the repose of this great continent, and who, I believe, would gladly accommodate differences upon almost any terms."

Though there is no news to communicate, famous Virginians are beginning to come in increasing numbers to the imposing establishment overlooking the Potomac. Patrick Henry has his eye on the stately *farmer*. The letters posted from Mt. Vernon by way of Alexandria reach farther and farther. Who is this farmer who writes so much to so many citizens dwelling so far away in the remotest colonies?

The British government has passed a Stamp Act. It had already passed the Navigation Acts and the Writs of Assistance. The colonies are going to be kept dependent, no matter what else occurs. They must ship in British bottoms. They must not manufacture products for their own markets. They must open their doors to any officer in the king's name who demands entrance to search their homes for smuggled goods.

The Mutiny Act is a hypocritical measure providing for a standing army of 10,000 men in America. The Crown says it intends to protect the helpless colonists against Indian outbreaks, but the

BRAGGADOCIO AT ITS WORST

colonists see through the measure and know that the standing army is designed to repress their liberties.

The Stamp Act (1765) goes too far. Those who disobey it shall be tried without a jury. Patrick Henry, a brilliant young lawyer, has reason for keeping his eye on Mt. Vernon. The farmer on the Potomac knows that back in 1215 the barons of England, led by Cardinal Stephen Langton, had demanded a charter of liberties, the Magna Charta, and that forty years later the gentry of England had demanded and received the right to elect representatives to parliament. This strange Virginia farmer knows all about the later Habeas Corpus Act and the Bill of Rights giving the Englishman real liberty, including control of his government and control of his taxation. He knows that no free man can be taxed, except by his own representatives.

He doubts that the Englishmen at home are superior to the Englishmen in America. He will resist the Stamp Act. He will write letters urging others to resist it. He will set about to establish an association of men devoted to resistance. He is a braggart who fumbles his words, using pompous Capital Letters where modest lower-case would render humbler service.

So until the Crown recognizes the injustice of

its folly there will be no more importations from England of articles burdened by a duty. The Philadelphians have come to this decision. They are spirited men, and right. Yes, there will be conventions in all parts of Virginia. Washington will stir up sentiment against importation throughout Fairfax County. He will go to Williamsburg and Richmond. He will act.

His letters are fearless. As early as 1769 he writes to Robert Carey & Company, London:

"If there are any articles contained in either of the respective invoices (paper only excepted) which are taxed by Act of Parliament for the purpose of raising a revenue in America, it is my express desire and request, that they may not be sent, as I have very heartily entered into an association not to import any article which now is, or hereafter shall be taxed for this purpose until the said act or acts are repealed. I am therefore particular in mentioning this matter as I am fully determined to adhere religiously to it, and may perhaps have wrote for some things unwittingly which may be under these circumstances."

In another letter written to London in 1770, he says:

"You will perceive, in looking over the several invoices, that some of the goods there required, are

BRAGGADOCIO AT ITS WORST

upon condition, that the act of Parliament imposing a duty on tea, paper, &c. for the purpose of raising a revenue in America, is totally repealed; and I beg the favor of you to be governed strictly thereby, as it will not be in my power to receive any articles contrary to our non-importation agreement, which I have subscribed, and shall religiously adhere to, and should, if it were, as I could wish it to be, ten times as strict."

This is mere braggadocio, but we haven't seen the half of it.

CHAPTER XIII

IMPERIOUS EGOTISM

COLONEL GEORGE MASON is Washington's neighbor and friend. They visit each other on horse-back, talk over the means of organizing opposition against the outrages of the Crown. The years of tranquillity at Mt. Vernon are galloping to a close. Washington is comfortable enough to stand any tax with a shrug, but a shrug is the one thing he can't understand. He does understand justice and knows that without justice there can be neither comfort nor peace. Peace and comfort are accidents to be legitimately enjoyed if honestly earned. Justice is fundamental. Without it all else is make-believe.

Colonel Mason agrees with Washington. A convention is called. He will assemble the people of Fairfax County to meet at Alexandria, July 18, 1774. Washington will preside, but the resolves which will be known throughout history as the Mason Resolves will be presented by Colonel Mason. Here indeed is egotism. The Resolves are actually written in Washington's own hand. They are Washington's Resolves, but Mason, not Wash-

IMPERIOUS EGOTISM

ington, will be linked with them till the end of time.

The two men on horse-back canter over the road to Alexandria with the soul of the Second Continental Congress in their saddles and the spirit of the Declaration of Independence in their hearts. The Mason Resolves are presented at the convention. The devil rageth. The history of nations is about to undergo its most violent change. The two men on horse-back, coming fresh from a farm at Mt. Vernon, have in their keeping the destiny of a new world.

It is the beginning of the end, and from this moment Martha and George will not again sit down to dinner by themselves during the coming twenty years.

Would lovers of Washington or defamers of Washington know how he treats this momentous issue? In his diary for 1774 four ridiculous lines dispose of the event.

It is not Washington's habit to picture his own conduct in odes or sonnets. Yet we might expect just a little display of vanity under circumstances so tremendous. The egotist, at once the despair, the consternation of his enemies, the glory and inspiration of his friends, sees fit to write only this:

> "July 17. Went to Pohick Church and returned to Dinner. Colo. Mason came in the afternoon and stayed all Night.

18. Went up to Alexandria to a Meeting of the County. Returnd in the Evening—Mr. Magowan with me."

The Boston Massacre of 1768; the suppression of the North Carolina Regulators of 1771; the Boston Tea Party of 1773, have been forgotten, but the Five Intolerable Acts; the closing of the Boston Port by Parliament; the annulling of the Massachusetts Charter; the odious Transportation Bill; the vicious Quartering Act, and the hypocritical Quebec Act, designed to prevent the Canadian Catholics from helping their Protestant neighbors in the colonies, have not been forgotten.

Washington went to Pohick Church and prayed, spent the afternoon with Colonel Mason on the Mason Resolves, kept Mason over-night at Mt. Vernon, went up to the Alexandria meeting and returned in the evening. How much was done and how much came of the doing is hidden away in this characteristic entry of Washington's diary, but, however deeply buried, it burns through the centuries like radium through flesh.

What strange gentlemen now pour in upon the Mt. Vernon farmer! Thomas Johnson, subsequently a member of the Second Continental Congress, William Paca, a destined signer of the Declaration of Independence, are in session with him.

IMPERIOUS EGOTISM

Immediately he is off to the famous convention at Williamsburg, where he rouses his colleagues with a single sentence: "I will raise one thousand men, subsist them at my own expense, and march myself at their head for the relief of Boston."

Of course he is elected, along with Peyton Randolph, Richard Henry Lee, Patrick Henry, Richard Bland, Benjamin Harrison, and Edmund Pendleton, as delegates from Virginia to the First Continental Congress, called to convene September, 1774, in Philadelphia. So he hurries home, for there is work to do. Colonel Mason, Patrick Henry and Edmund Pendleton, August 30, "came in the evening and stay'd all night."

> "August 31. All the above gentlemen dined here; after which with Colo. Pendleton and Mr. Henry, I set out on my journey for Phila."

And what a journey!

In November he is back home at Mt. Vernon, mustering brave spirits into the Prince William County Independent Company and the Fairfax County Independent Company.

In January, 1775, he is drilling independents at Alexandria, buying eight quarter casks of powder, buying muskets.

In March, 1775, he starts off for the Virginia

Convention at Richmond, where he is elected delegate to the Second Continental Congress. There are more purchases of powder.

May 4 he sets off for Philadelphia again. May 9 he sups at Mr. Joseph Read's. Samuel Curwen kept a journal where we find, May 9, 1775, "passed the evening at Joseph Read's in company with Col. Washington, a fine figure and of a most easy and agreeable address."

Remember the casual description of the egotist at this time—the egotist who says nothing about himself but who buys forty more muskets May 24, 1775.

CHAPTER XIV

DULL, SULLEN, GLOOMY, GRAVE

JUNE 15, 1775, the egotist writes twelve words in his diary: "Dined at Burnes' in the Field. Spent the Eveng. on a committee." What would the ordinary man have done in recording such an event as occurred on that memorable day, June 15, 1775? Washington spent the evening on a committee but the Continental Congress devoted the day to destiny, unanimously electing "George Washington, Esquire, General and Commander-in-Chief of all the forces raised, or to be raised, by the United Colonies."

The committee spent the night drafting rules and regulations for the government of the army. It took four days to engross and sign the commission. Washington casually disposes of these four days, the evenings of three of which he spends at his lodgings, the fourth at the lodgings of Thomas Lynch, a delegate from South Carolina. There are no more entries until 1781. The commander-in-chief is too busy with the enemy to glorify his deeds. He disposes of them in twelve words and, were the events

GREATEST OF MEN—WASHINGTON

not elsewhere written in fire, we would know nothing of them.

Yet the 1926 biographers insinuate that he wanted to be king. He wanted a noble title—an extravagantly noble title. He was an egotist even as a boy, showing off before company with a map of his own making. As first president he wanted to be grand. His snobbery had to be stepped on. Because he was crossed in his high mightiness he became grim, sullen, awe-inspiring.

Go back to the picture of Samuel Curwen, "a fine figure, and of a most easy and agreeable address." Now consult "Jefferson and Hamilton," by Claude G. Bowers.

By trials, treacheries, hardships, desertions, the inaction of the Congress that had made him commander-in-chief, the utter chaos that followed the war when the victorious colonies were engaged in rivalries and jealousies threatening self-destruction, Washington had all but lost confidence in the mob. He knew at least what not to depend upon. He was fighting for the future of his native land, his love for which was a passion scarcely to be understood by self-seekers, egotists and ambitious men.

Bowers makes the gravity of the later Washington understandable.

"The great man had entered upon his physical decline when he assumed the Presidency, and many

DULL, SULLEN, GLOOMY, GRAVE

found him changed—'pale, almost cadavorous,' his deportment 'invariably grave,' his sobriety barely stopping short of sadness. Even at Mrs. Washington's drawing-rooms, when beautiful girls swarmed about him, his face never softened to a smile. It is more than probable that he was not a little bored by the artificial restraints imposed upon him by his advisors on etiquette, who had aristocratic notions of the dignity of his position. Both Hamilton and Adams were responsible for planning his isolation from the people."

Maclay, who dined at least twice with the President, writes: "The President seemed to bear in his countenance a settled aspect of melancholy. No cheering ray of convivial sunshine broke through the cloudy gloom of settled seriousness."

Again the same man writes of one of these dinners: "The best of the kind I was ever at. The most solemn dinner ever I sat at. Not a health drank, scarce a word said until the cloth was taken away."

We don't have to imagine that Washington was bored with the artificial court life by which he was surrounded. The very Tories who had opposed him had now become the important people, the society leaders, the wonder and mortification, the irony of the old savage days of heroism and valor, self-sacrifice and simplicity. We know he was bored. Fif-

GREATEST OF MEN—WASHINGTON

teen times during his two terms he managed to get away from it all for short trips to Mt. Vernon, where he and Martha could be themselves *on a farm!*

And now they tell us he would have been a Colossus if they would have allowed him so much glory. They tell us Hamilton mortally offended him, yet we know that he did everything in his power to compose the deadly animosities existing between Hamilton and Thomas Jefferson. He begged them to stop their quarreling, and even schemed to bring them together with himself in a cotton factory, so that their hatred of each other might be forgotten and a new friendship born.

Great men have ever been assailed. The *American Mercury*, October 2, 1800, dwelling on contributions made by Jefferson to the Church and to needy clergymen, came to his assistance with this:

"Thus while Mr. Jefferson is practising the blessed religion of Jesus Christ by acts of charity and benevolence, these political parsons are abusing that holy religion and profaning the temple of God by fulminating lies and slander against Mr. Jefferson."

From political enemies almost any charge may be expected, but Washington now has no political enemies. How, then, are we to account for the lies and slanders fulminated against him? He wasn't even a good general.

DULL, SULLEN, GLOOMY, GRAVE

"As a military leader he was deficient in ideas. He lacked originality. His tactics were thoroughly out of tune with the colonial character.

"The American of 1776 was a marksman without an equal in the world. His thought was always of putting a bullet where it ought to go. He liked to fight behind trees or rocks. Through instruction, discipline and flogging Washington attempted to turn these sharp-shooting rangers into an army composed of lines and squares."

Here are lies. Even as a youngster with Braddock, Washington begged that blundering idiot to send his men behind rocks and trees. The fool refused and was mowed down. Washington, the youngster, had the wisdom of a general even then. He did not try "to whip an army into shape with a lash." He whipped traitors, scoundrels and the dissolute instead of putting them to death. His whippings, rare enough, were designed to save a nation. That he saved that nation is admitted even by the 1926 biographers, who apparently know as little of generalship as they know of history and nothing at all of the man whose biography they have presumed to write.

CHAPTER XV

A GRAND OPERA GENERAL

IS Washington a general? He is about to enter the war. Congress is torn by the bitterest divisions. "It is almost impossible," writes Adams, "to move anything but you instantly see private friendships and enmities, and provincial views and prejudices, intermingle in the consultation. Every important step is opposed and a large amount of jealousy and suspicion displayed."

Zubly, delegate from Georgia, asserts that "a republican government is little better than government of devils."

New England is under fire. The New England troops are turbulent, insubordinate, untrained. Washington, the Virginian, is unknown to them. Massachusetts, of all the provinces, is the most revolutionary. She has her own little pool of officers torn by petty, heterogeneous, feeble and ragged jealousies and ambitions.

Will they accept the supreme command of the stranger from Virginia? The non-combatants constitute an undecided and fluctuating majority, nearly all of whose influential members are strongly

A GRAND OPERA GENERAL

on the side of the Crown. Many of them industrious, money-loving, shrewd and prosperous have been making fortunes. They fear all the comforts of their little world will vanish.

Washington's equipment for war is notoriously inadequate. He pulls fifty cannon down from Ticonderoga on ox-sleds. When he arrives at Cambridge the troops available for service number 14,500. They will have to guard a line twelve miles in length held by 9,000 trained regulars.

The colonies are urged to send recruits. The bombastic Charles Lee announces that in three or four months an efficient army of 100,000 infantry will be available. A paltry 5,000 represents a month's recruiting. Each body of troops is raised under the laws of its own colony and the men refuse to accept any regulations imposed by the Congress. Even the officers appointed by Congress are not acceptable to the troops, who rebel violently and announce that they will serve only under such officers as they please, and of their own choice.

General Schuyler goes so far as to say that "the troops from Connecticut will not bear with a general from another colony."

The birth throes of the new nation are paroxysms. Petty quarrels about rank, and pay, and service are incessant. Mercenaries postpone enlistment in the belief that the great public distress will compel the

GREATEST OF MEN—WASHINGTON

Congress to offer large bounties for service. The men who come reluctantly to the colors enlist for short periods only. There is no 1917 draft for death and eternity. The Connecticut troops enlist to December. When December comes the entire outfit, 5,000 strong, abandon the field. Not one of them will re-enlist. All appeals are in vain. Their desertion will bring absolute ruin upon the American cause. To hell with the American cause. Congress will grant no bounties and the scale of pay is less than ordinary employment will yield. Better to be a pig-farmer, a peddler or a tinker than an unpaid patriot; a lover of husks than a nation-builder.

Washington himself writes, November 28, 1775;

"Such a dearth of public spirit, and such want of virtue, such stock-jobbing and fertility in all the low arts to obtain advantages in this great change of military arrangement I never saw before, and pray God's mercy I may never be witness to again. Such a mercenary spirit pervades the whole that I should not be at all surprised at any disaster that may happen."

Again he writes: "It grieves me to see so little of that patriotic spirit which I was taught to believe was characteristic of this people."

Yes, the most formidable of the difficulties Washington has to encounter are in his own camp. He

A GRAND OPERA GENERAL

has to extend furloughs as far as fifty men to a regiment at the very time he needs them most, in order to keep them at all. Yet with his wretched forces, such as they are, he will compel General Gates to evacuate Boston. By night he fortifies Dorchester Heights. At sunrise the trained British troops are astounded to find entrenchments overlooking the city where the night before there had been none.

It is March 17. The American countersign is "St. Patrick." Washington takes the city. General Howe, with 9,000 men and a thousand Tories, escapes by boat to Halifax, where he plans an attack on New York. He will proceed by water to Staten Island. There he will be met by reinforcements from England.

If they can command "Hudson's River" they will be able to command "Hudson's valley." Dominating New York and the East River, they will cut the colonies in two, preventing communication between Massachusetts and Virginia. Can Washington's doubtful generalship see through the scheme? Will he abandon the now useless Boston and head for Manhattan? Will he find but an eighth of the men promised him by Congress?

The British are 30,000 strong. The Mt. Vernon farmer is merely a gesture, a will-o'-the-wisp, an airy threat. At least two of his companions, Generals Charles Lee and Conway, secretly sneer. Even now they are trying to destroy him. But Washington has penetrated the British plan. He hastens to the rag-tags and bobtails assembled at New York. He is building entrenchments on Long Island. Desertions, jealousies, quarrels, continue without abatement. Smallpox breaks out among his troops. He has nearly 9,000 men, most of whom are in the depths of discouragement. They are badly clad, poorly armed, without military experience. The British drop 16,000 trained and disciplined troops on Long Island. The Americans are hemmed in. Attacked from front and rear, 1,100 of his men are killed or wounded. The British are equipped with deadly artillery. Washington hasn't a single company of cavalry. The morrow will intensify the slaughter.

By bringing up their fleet between Brooklyn and New York, the British will make escape impossible. Moreover, Clinton is threatening to send part of his army across the Sound. The menace is imminent.

There is a high wind and a strong ebb-tide. They are so close to Washington that the blows of their pick-axes can be distinctly heard. Perhaps Washington prays for a fog, his only hope. At any rate, about 2 in the morning the fog descends. The British fleet is about to enter the East River. The continentals are in a pocket. The jig is up.

A GRAND OPERA GENERAL

Somehow fishermen have been inextricably mixed up with destiny. Many of the Marblehead fishermen, to their glory forever, had raillied to Washington's call. At hand were smacks and flat-bottomed boats, smelling of fish and a thousand voyages. Before morning the fog, the Marblehead fishermen and the smelly boats have enabled Washington, despite the wind and the rough waters, to abandon his entrenchments, to cross the East River with nearly all his provisions, horses, wagons and ammunition. The retreat is accomplished without panic, without noise, without betrayal. Colonel Glover, who belonged to Marblehead, will never be forgotten. The Marblehead fishermen will live forever. They have helped make Washington's retreat one of the very greatest of his achievements.

Now he is on the other side, exhausted by anguish and the fatigue of the operation. It is utterly impossible to put his numbed hand to a pen. He cannot report immediately to Congress. The slaughter occurred midway between August 27-28, 1776. Washington knows he must retreat further up the shore, into Westchester County. The British have possession of Long Island. Howe is getting ready to fall upon the broken and exhausted Americans.

After four days of frenzied activity Washington takes his quill to make delayed report. This is what he writes:

GREATEST OF MEN—WASHINGTON

"Since Monday scarce any of us have been out of the lines, till our passage across the East River was effected. For forty-eight hours preceding that, I had hardly been off my horse, and never closed my eyes; so that I was quite unfit to write or dictate till this morning."

Later Thomas Jefferson referred meanly to Washington's "waning mental powers and his advancing years." For his failure to remember Washington's 104 months of sustained hardship it is difficult to forgive even that great and useful man.

September 2 Washington writes again:

"Our situation is truly distressing. The check our detachments sustained on the 27th ultimo, has dispirited too great a proportion of our troops, and filled their minds with apprehension and despair. Till of late I had no doubt in my own mind of defending this place (New York); nor should I have yet, if the men would do their duty. But this I despair of."

September 13 three British frigates and a forty-gun ship sail up the East River pouring a continuous fire into New York. General Howe wants New York. Washington is driven north as far as Harlem. He carries away all New York's church bells to be converted into cannon. He writes:

"Almost every villainy and rascality is daily practised by the American troops with impunity. The

A GRAND OPERA GENERAL

American cause is lost. The militia are dismayed, intractable and impatient to return. Great numbers have gone off, in some instances almost by whole regiments, by half ones, and by companies at a time. Their want of discipline and refusal of almost every kind of restraint, their humors and intolerable caprice, their entire disregard of that order and subordination necessary to the well-being of an army, their abominable desertions, etc., etc."

There is no need to prolong Washington's agony of spirit. He will continue fortifying Harlem Heights, but he will also draw his army further north into White Plains at the west side of the Bronx River. His operations will be so well covered up that the British will not suspect the truth until they are no longer able to interfere. His generalship is about to be made manifest to the entire world. The French Minister M. Gerard will write to his government:

"I will now say only, that I have formed as high an opinion of the powers of Washington's mind, his moderation, his patriotism and his virtues, as I had before from common report conceived of his military talents, and of the incalculable services he has rendered to his country."

Though Washington will savagely rebuke him for it, Colonel Lewis Nicola will propose for him the title of King. But let us see this general.

CHAPTER XVI

ABSURD ANTICS ON THE DELAWARE

TO know Washington we must see him under stress. "The abandoned and profligate part of our army," he writes, "lost to every sense of honor and virtue, as well as their country's good, are by rapine and plunder spreading ruin and terror wherever they go. They are thereby making themselves infinitely more to be dreaded than the common enemy they are come to oppose."

The utmost penalty he is empowered to inflict is thirty-nine lashes. Of course the 1926 biographers discover cruelty!

But generalship? Washington will not yield to hopelessness. He will dog the British. Avoiding general action, he will indulge in slight skirmishes. He still holds Fort Washington, but realizes the necessity of withdrawing even here. General Greene determines otherwise. The British storm the fort, capturing 2,700 Americans with all their artillery and military stores. Another harassing loss. The surrounding country will now be possessed. Washington has written: "It will not be prudent to hazard the stores and men at Mt. Wash-

ABSURD ANTICS ON THE DELAWARE

ington; but as you are on the spot I leave it to you to give such orders as you may judge best."

Greene knows better than Washington and the result is another hell.

So Washington retreats into New Jersey. His 8,000 troops have dwindled to 4,000. General Howe pursues him. Fort Lee is assailed. The Americans are driven westward. The British are cleaning up in all sectors. Winter is approaching. Washington actually hungers for a mere handful, five or six hundred Indians. There is no hope of success, but one man who, though he can write frantically of despair, cannot act as if he knows what he is talking about. That man is Washington.

He has left General Charles Lee with a body of troops on the east side of "Hudson's River." It is time for Lee to join him. Lee secretly hates Washington. He will not obey. For reasons never disclosed, still known only to himself and God, he dallies where he is until it's too late. Capriciously he crosses the Hudson to the Jersey side and is promptly captured, confessing to the British that "the game is nearly at an end."

This tragedy strikes new terror into the American army. It is not enough that its discouragement is already complete; woe must be piled upon woe. Washington is closely pursued by vastly superior forces under Howe. He retreats to Newark.

GREATEST OF MEN—WASHINGTON

Driven from Newark, he tries to make a stand at Brunswick. His deplorable situation cannot be described. Moreover, Cornwallis is about to join the pursuit.

Abandoning Brunswick, he heads for Princeton. Cornwallis enters the struggle, seizes every advantage and presses him hard. Now he flees to Trenton and gets as far as the Pennsylvania side of the Delaware River. The majority of the non-combatants along the way are utterly indifferent or have become actually hostile to his cause. He writes frankly, December 5, about these "late disgraces." December 12, he writes that a great part of the continental troops have insisted on abandoning him.

"I hoped to receive a reinforcement from the militia of the State of New Jersey sufficient to check the further progress of the enemy. The inhabitants, either from fear or disaffection, almost to a man refused to turn out."

Again he writes: "With a handful of men we have been pushed through the Jerseys without being able to make the smallest opposition."

The inhabitants refuse the least aid, actually exulting at the approach of the enemy and Washington's own misfortunes. Was there ever such a man?

Entering the war he had written his brother, John Augustine: "It is my full intention to devote my life

ABSURD ANTICS ON THE DELAWARE

and fortune in the cause we are engaged in." Was word ever so sacredly kept?

Ignoring the losses due to treachery, he has taken every boat of every conceivable kind along the Delaware shore for 70 miles and has got to the Pennsylvania side. The British for the moment are baffled. They will wait for the river to freeze over. They will cross on the ice. It is Christmas. Six days remain. For these six days he will at least have something that will be called an army. December 31 the term of enlistment of the greater part of his troops will expire. The day before Christmas he writes the president of the Congress: "I have not the most distant prospect of retaining them a moment longer than the last of this month, notwithstanding the most pressing solicitations and the obvious necessity for it."

So the 1926 biographers will belittle his generalship. The man is insane. The Delaware is full of ice. A rotten sleet shells him even from heaven. Who could dream of attacking an overwhelmingly superior enemy under such abominable conditions? Washington, with his expiring army, having but six days to live, will cross the Delaware through the floating ice, through the sleet.

He will attack the British flag and Hessian hirelings on the other side.

So he does.

GREATEST OF MEN—WASHINGTON

The surprise attack is complete. Two of his men are frozen to death. Two of his officers are killed.

The attack is so utterly impossible, so unthinkable, that he finds in his hands a thousand prisoners and the very ammunition and stores he needs.

The effect of this coup is electrical. The desponding, wavering, hostile populace cannot resist such skill, such courage, such glorious maneuver. Philadelphia is saved—for the time. Pennsylvania at once rallies a large force who join Washington immediately. His own troops, to whom he appeals as never man appealed before, do not laugh at the artificial ivories showing through the haggard lips of their chief. They consent to stick with him for another six weeks. A bounty of ten dollars helps a little to turn the tide.

So he speedily moves to Trenton and just as speedily occupies it. A tremendous British force has been sent to dispatch the insolent Virginian. He evades the British and, wholly unexpected attacks Princeton, where he defeats three regiments. Now he has the enemy falling back. He drives them to Brunswick and recovers the greater part of New Jersey. The inhabitants who sneered only a month before are now mad about this man.

The militia will join him. Recruits pour in. The manifest superiority of his generalship as he pounds to pieces a superior army of trained veterans works

ABSURD ANTICS ON THE DELAWARE

a revolution of deep and lasting sentiment in the hearts of his former foes.

This is not rhetoric, it is generalship. Washington's tactics are now spontaneously engendered. There is little time for councils of war. He is thinking of dying in defeat, if needs be, but he is thinking more of living, maneuvering, fighting, conquering. The thought has become brazen. Its very desperation taps resources deeper than nature and inspires action so startling that Frederick the Great, analyzing Washington's achievements in the ten days between December 25th and January 4th, pronounced them to be "the most brilliant recorded in military annals."

What if Major-General Francis Vinton Greene quotes Moncure D. Conway to prove that Frederick the Great never said anything of the kind? Greene himself extends those wonderful ten days to fourteen more wonderful days and in his enthusiasm compares Washington's reckless exposure in the hand-to-hand encounter as on a par with that of Napoleon at Lodi. Greene doesn't like Frederick, but admits that the astounding movement at once and forever established Washington's reputation as a soldier.

CHAPTER XVII

BRITISH AND JESUIT CALUMNIES

IT is not necessary to follow Washington through the war, but it is necessary to refer to his diary for May, 1781. The brilliance of his campaign when he turns the tide of battle on the banks of the Delaware is not to insure him against further disaster, further hardship. He is never to be free from gross and bitter trial. After six years of suspense, sustained endurance against overwhelming odds, intolerable sufferings, treachery and desertions, the fearless, the most fearless general of all wars, the one general who commanded always from the front line, never from the rear, writes this, May, 1781:

"Instead of having Magazines filled with munition, we have a scanty pittance scattered here and there in the different States. Instead of having our Arsenals well supplied with Military Stores, they are poorly provided, and the Workmen all leaving them. Instead of having the various articles of Field equipage in readiness to deliver, the Quarter Master General is but now applying to the several States to provide these things.

"Instead of having a regular System of transportation established upon credit—or funds in the Quar-

BRITISH AND JESUIT CALUMNIES

ter Master's hands . . . we have neither the one nor the other . . . and are daily and hourly oppressing the people—souring their tempers—and alienating their affections. . . . Scarce any State in the Union has, at this hour, an eighth part of its quota in the Field. Instead of having everything in readiness to take the Field we have nothing. Instead of having the prospect of a glorious offensive campaign before us, we have a bewildered and gloomy defensive one."

Washington has been fighting six years. These words of his cover the glory of the man. Without eloquence they disclose what he has had to endure and how he has endured it. Some noble Britisher can always be depended upon to state the truth fearlessly and gloriously when all his fellows seem to be conspiring with darkness and deceit. There has never been a British crisis without its champion of right against might, its champion of truth against falsehood, its champion of virtue against infamy.

The British historian, Lecky, famed for the coldness and justice of his judgments, tells the truth about Washington. "His great modesty and taciturnity kept him in the background, both in the Provincial Legislature and in the Continental Congress. Though his voice was scarcely ever heard in debate, his superiority was soon felt."

Lecky accepts at face value the words of Patrick

GREATEST OF MEN—WASHINGTON

Henry: "If you speak of solemn information or sound judgment, Colonel Washington is unquestionably the greatest man in the Congress."

But permit Lecky to go on:

"To the appointment of Washington, is due the ultimate success of the American Revolution. His military reputation steadily rose and before the end of the struggle he had outlived all rivalry, and almost all envy. He possessed to an eminent degree not only the common courage of a soldier, but also that much rarer courage which can endure long-continued suspense, bear the weight of great responsibility, and encounter the risks of misrepresentation and unpopularity. For years, and usually in the neighborhood of superior forces, he commanded a perpetually fluctuating army, almost wholly destitute of discipline and respect for authority, torn by the most violent personal and provincial jealousies, wretchedly armed, wretchedly clothed, and sometimes in imminent danger of starvation.

"Unsupported for the most part by the population and incessantly thwarted by the jealousy of Congress, he kept his army together by a combination of skill, firmness, patience, and judgment which has rarely been surpassed. In civil as in military life, he was pre-eminent among his contemporaries for the clearness and soundness of his judgment, for his perfect moderation and self-control, for the quiet dignity and the indomitable firmness with which he pursued every path deliberately chosen. Of all the great men in history he was the most invariably ju-

BRITISH AND JESUIT CALUMNIES

dicious, and there is scarcely a rash word, or action, or judgment recorded of him.

"He had keen sensibilities and strong passions but his power of self-command never failed him, and no act of his public life can be traced to personal caprice, ambition or resentment. In the despondency of long-continued failure, in the elation of sudden success, when his soldiers were deserting by hundreds, when malignant plots were formed against his reputation, amid the constant quarrels, rivalries and jealousies of his subordinates, in the dark hour of national ingratitude, and in the midst of the most universal and intoxicating flattery, he was always the same calm, wise, just, and single-minded man, pursuing the course which he believed to be right, without fear or favor or fanaticism.

"He valued very highly fortune, position and reputation, but at the command of duty he was ready to risk and sacrifice them all. He carried into public life the severest standards of private morals.

"It was at first the constant dread of large sections of the American people, that if the old Government were overthrown, they would fall into the hands of military adventurers, and undergo the yoke of military despotism. It was mainly the transparent integrity of the character of Washington that dispelled the fear. It was always known by his friends, and it was soon acknowledged by the whole nation and by the English themselves, that in Washington America had found a leader who could be induced by no earthly motive to tell a falsehood, or to break an engagement, or to commit any dishon-

GREATEST OF MEN—WASHINGTON

orable act. There is scarcely another instance in history of such a man having reached and maintained the highest position in the convulsions of civil war and of a great popular agitation."

Let Paul L. Blakely, a Jesuit priest, say this:

"The world, then, can never forget Washington, but it may be that future generations will not know what manner of man he was. Made the advocate of policies which he abhorred and the embodiment of principles which he disowned, he may grow into a myth. The devil's advocate and the panegyrist are abroad, and each enshrouds his majestic figure with a cloak of unreality, hiding the man we wish to know.

"Great leaders are not raised up merely for the enlightenment of their own times. Raised aloft they are beacons to the generations that come after them. We gain nothing and may lose all by striving to make them what they were not. Smart paragraphs, brilliant periods, and an air of sophistication, are offered in place of careful research and discriminating evaluations. Washington has not escaped their desecrating pens."

CHAPTER XVIII

UTTERLY DEVOID OF SENTIMENT

IN 1787 Washington, a delegate from Virginia, attends the convention at Philadelphia that formulates the United States Constitution. Leaving his crops and experiments he crosses from Mt. Vernon a little after sunrise headed for Baltimore, where we find him, Thursday, May 10, at the Fountain Tavern.

Friday, May 11, he sets out *before breakfast* and rides twelve miles to Skirrett's Tavern. Please remember the ride and the breakfast, otherwise you will never know Washington. Something of profound significance, related to the ride and the breakfast, will follow in due place. At night he lodges at the Ferry, at Havre de Gras.

Saturday, May 12, with difficulty he crosses the Susquehanna. *Without breakfast*. Again remember. At the Ferry House on the East side he gets his hoe cakes, honey and coffee. Dining at the Head of Elk after half a day's journey, he lodges for the night at Patrick O'Flynn's Sign of the Ship.

Arriving in Philadelphia he seeks immediately

GREATEST OF MEN—WASHINGTON

Benjamin Franklin. The work of the Revolution has been done. Yet as far as Washington's diary is concerned there is not one line, not one word indicating he had a part in it greater than any of his companions in arms.

No vainglory, no sense of personal achievement, no bitter reference to defeat, betrayal, hardship, tragedy, no exultation over victory. No futile complaint when there are few men, little food, no powder.

In the silence of that diary somebody else might just as well have done the things that were done. Nowhere in the history of mankind is there such another record of modesty and self-effacement.

In all the excitement of the Constitutional Convention, Washington, after an absence from home of four months and fourteen days, speaks of little else but the taverns where daily he drinks tea and dines.

However turbulent the sessions, his own mind is steeped in tranquillity and is so completely master of its moods that he is able to set down this extraordinary note:

"That it (buckwheat) is considered as an excellent food for horses, to puff and give them their first fat, Milch cattle, Sheep, and Hogs, and also for fatting Beeves.

"To do which, 2 quarts of Buck Wheat Meal,

UTTERLY DEVOID OF SENTIMENT

half a peck of Irish Potatoes at the commencement, to be reduced as the appetite of the beasts decrease or in other words as they encrease in flesh. Mixed and given three times a day is fully competent. That Buck Wheat Meal made into a wash is most excellent to lay on fat upon hogs, but it must be hardened by feeding them some time afterwards with Corn. And that this Meal and Potatoes mixed is very good for Colts that are weaning."

This information he obtains from some farmers whom he observes working and with whom he enters into conversation as he "rid over the whole old Cantonment of the American Army of the Winter, 1777 and 8, visited the Works wch. were in Ruins; and the Incampments in woods where the grounds had not been cultivated." What a picture of the lonely rider revisiting the *whole* scene of earlier tragedy, too full of mixed emotions to give his experience a single word. He hastens to Buck Wheat!

His mind is full of the past and occupied with the present. The nation is really being born and he is presiding at its birth, yet inns, taverns, tea and farming oust everything else from the diary of this man of granite. One of his Postilion boys, Paris, is sick, so he gets Dr. John Jones to attend him. Only this and High Mass at the Romish Church, St. Mary's, and nothing more.

Out of the convention he is at the City Tavern

GREATEST OF MEN—WASHINGTON

dining or being dined. If we don't find him at Dr. Franklin's home drinking tea we must look for him at the Indian Queen Tavern, or at Mr. Bartram's Botanical Gardens.

We find him at the ordination of two gentlemen deacons by Bishop William White, the first Protestant Episcopal Bishop of Pennsylvania, or at the quarterly meeting of the Friendly Sons of St. Patrick at the City Tavern. Now he is at Gray's Ferry Tavern, three miles down the Schuylkill River.

At Epples Tavern he dines with the State Society of Cincinnati. Several times we find him at the Cold Spring and to the play at the Southwark Theatre.

Friday, August 2, 1787, in company with Robert Morris and his lady and Gouvr. Morris he goes on an evening fishing party but catches no fish. The following morning he catches some perch. What an exaggerating mountebank!

Tuesday, August 7, he actually refuses to drink tea for the first and last time of his recorded history. He had been drinking no other beverage throughout the convention. Tea! Tea! Tea! Here is a merry drinker indeed! America is afire! He drinks tea!

Sunday, August 19, he rides up to the White Marsh Tavern, 12 miles north of Philadelphia, from whence the Continental Army marched at the

UTTERLY DEVOID OF SENTIMENT

close of the Brandywine-Germantown campaign to its memorable winter quarters at Valley Forge. Sentiment overcomes him and he says: "I traversed my old Incampment, and contemplated on the dangers which threatened the American Army at that place," He is alone—traversing his old encampment—this unsentimental, unimaginative, prosy and unfeeling man! Twice we have caught him at this sentimental business; both times alone!

All through August and September he attends the convention, drinks tea, writes letters, dines, and awaits the striking off of printed copies of the Constitution which it is proposed to offer to the people.

Monday, September 17, the business being closed, he goes with the members to the City Tavern, where all take a cordial leave of each other.

So with chariot and horses he departs, Wednesday, September 19, for home, stopping on the way at the Head of Elk, Havre de Gras, Skirrett's Tavern twelve miles short of Baltimore, and the Widow Ball's.

By March 4, 1789, Washington, knowing that he cannot escape election as president of the United States under the new Constitution, seeks a loan of £500 from Captain Richard Conway of Alexandria, a thing "I never expected to be driven to—that is to borrow money on interest."

April 16 the first President writes:

GREATEST OF MEN—WASHINGTON

"About ten o'clock I bade adieu to Mt. Vernon, to private life, and to domestic felicity, and with a mind oppressed with more anxious and painful sensations than I have words to express, set out for New York in company with Mr. Thomson and Col. Humphreys, with the best disposition to render service to my country in obedience to its calls, but with less hope of answering its expectations."

Mere quackery, nothing more!

CHAPTER XIX

WHAT THEY CALL TOASTING

NOW we know something of the inns and taverns, something of the home of Washington, something of the houses of the old colonial days. But what about Washington's own food habits and the dishes prepared at Mt. Vernon and served at the inns and taverns throughout the country?

At all the cross-roads sprang up the ordinaries or hostelries of the day, and here the men of the countryside would gather and over the punch bowl or the wine bottle make merry. As a youngster Washington's ledger account shows expenditures for a bottle of Rhenish at Mitchell's 1s. 3d., and again "to cash in part for a Bowl of fruit punch 1s. 7½d."

During the Revolution all his aides live with him at headquarters. He calls them "my family." If he has plenty Sepawn and milk he is content. At his camp at Valley Forge *one* very special dinner consists of vegetables, roast beef, lamb, chicken, salad dressed with vinegar, green peas, puddings, and a kind of tart, most everything served on the

GREATEST OF MEN—WASHINGTON

same plate. There were no other such dinners during that terrible ordeal.

On another occasion Washington writes of Valley Forge in delightful irony:

"Since our arrival at this happy spot, we have had a ham (sometimes a shoulder) of Bacon, to grace the head of the Table; a piece of roast Beef adorned the foot; a dish of beans or greens (almost imperceptible) decorates the center. When the cook has a mind to cut a figure we have two Beef-steak pyes, or dishes of crab, one on each side of the center dish, dividing the space and reducing the distance between dish and dish to about six feet, which without them would be near twelve feet apart. Of late he has the surprising sagacity to discover, that apples will make pyes; and it's a question, if, in the violence of his efforts, we do not get one of apples, instead of having both of Beef-steaks."

The plates were iron. The human reaction pure gold!

As President, Washington gives formal dinners. First there is soup, then fish roasted and broiled, meats, fowl, game. The desserts are apple pyes, pudding, ice cream, jellies, then watermelon, muskmelons, apples, peaches, nuts. Afterwards coffee upstairs.

Bradbury describes one of the President's dinners. "There was an elegant variety of roast beef,

WHAT THEY CALL TOASTING

veal, turkey, duck, fowls, hams, puddings, jellies, oranges, apples, nuts, almonds, figs, raisins, and a variety of wines and punch."

At Mt. Vernon there was a small roasted pig, boiled leg of lamb, roasted fowls, beef, peas, lettuce, cucumbers, artichokes, venison, goose, duck, herring, shad, carp, turnips, parsnips, peaches, pears, apples, grapes, puddings, tarts, tea, coffee, port, Madeira, hard cider, cherry bounce, whiskey, rum, champagne. Not all together.

There were many barbeques, clam bakes and turtle dinners. Samuel Stearns tells us that Washington breakfasted at 7 o'clock on three small Indian hoe cakes and as many dishes of tea. Custis is more explicit, relating that "Indian cakes, honey and tea formed his temperate repast." Of course these men were mere falsifiers. Both reveal that at dinner "he ate heartily, but was not particular in his diet, with the exception of fish, of which he was excessively fond. He took sparingly of dessert, drank a home-made beverage, and from four to five glasses of Madeira wine." Stearns says "he dines, commonly, on a single dish, and drinks from half a pint to a pint of Madeira wine. This, with one small glass of punch, a draft of beer, and two dishes of tea taken half an hour before sun-setting, constitutes his whole sustenance till the next day."

Ashbell Green relates that at the state banquets

GREATEST OF MEN—WASHINGTON

during the presidency "he generally dined on one single dish." All this has been commonly known for more than a century. Later authorities have added nothing to the fact. They have written headlines.

In 1782 Richard Varick wrote: "General Washington dines with me tomorrow; he is exceedingly fond of salt fish. . . . If you could conveniently lend me as much fish as would serve a pretty large company it will oblige me. Could you not prevail upon somebody to catch some trout for me early tomorrow morning?"

Custis, favored of men, tells us that salt codfish was Washington's regular Sunday dinner, and that a second liking was honey. His ledger mentions purchases of honey. In 1789 his sister wrote: "When I last had the Pleasure of seeing you I observed your fondness for Honey; I have got a large Pot of very fine in the comb, which I shall send by the first opportunity."

Besides the nuts raised on his own plantation, he bought hazelnuts and shellbarks by the barrel. In 1792 he wrote his overseer to "tell house Frank I expect he will lay up a more plenteous store of the black common walnuts than he usually does."

The Prince de Broglie recorded that "at dessert he eats an enormous quantity of nuts, and when the conversation is entertaining he keeps eating through

WHAT THEY CALL TOASTING

a couple of hours, from time to time giving sundry healths, according to the English and American custom. It is what they call toasting."

From his own confession we know he was fond of spices of all sorts, including mustard, nutmeg, cinnamon and pepper.

Anne Hollingsworth Wharton describes the Mt. Vernon breakfast as consisting of "fresh fish, bacon or ham with eggs, corn cakes, honey and coffee, which Martha Washington delighted to set before her husband." Friday evenings Lady Washington entertained at receptions with her own plum cake, tea and coffee. Ice creams and candies were commonly served. It was all uproarious debauchery. Greater wickedness no man hath seen!

CHAPTER XX

CONTEMPT FOR THE POPULACE

DURING the colonial and post-revolutionary days we have found George Washington lodged for the night or dining at scores of wayside inns, taverns and ordinaries, many of them fancifully named. Perhaps they lacked the charm of the more famous English taverns and celebrated inns. Certainly they lacked the crazy beams and rafters, the age-old oaken boards and carved oaken doors that delighted Kit Marlowe, Ben Jonson, Will Shakespeare, and Walter Raleigh. But they were none the less real inns and taverns, and Washington himself gives us the best possible evidence of their number and enterprise.

Doubtless he was familiar with Samuel Johnson's verses written at an inn at Henley:

"Here, waiter! take my sordid ore,
    Which lacqueys else might hope to win;
It buys, what courts have not in store;
    It buys me freedom at an inn.

"Whoe'r has travel'd life's dull round,
    Where'er his stages may have been,
May sigh to think he still has found
    The warmest welcome, at an inn."

CONTEMPT FOR THE POPULACE

It may be said that stern necessity, not sentimental response to their enticements, led him to knock at the doors of these establishments. But his own diary affords ample proof that where there was no necessity at all he sought their comfort and entertainment on many occasions.

All the way from Portsmouth, N. H., to Savannah, Ga., and throughout his difficult journeys westward, he found but one inn where no accommodations were made for horses. Now and again he noted that the entertainment afforded was indifferent, thus indicating his own experience of their hospitality had taught him to expect more than these exceptions had to offer.

There was nothing surprising in the humanness of this man. In all ages the tavern and the inn have given expression to man's humanness. Witness the Ruba'iyat of Omar Khayyam:

"Before the phantom of False morning died,
  Methought a Voice within the Tavern cried,
    'When all the Temple is prepared within,
  'Why nods the drowsy Worshipper outside?'"

"And, as the Cock crew, those who stood before
The Tavern shouted—'Open then the Door!
  'You know how little while we have to stay,
  'And, once departed, may return no more.'"

GREATEST OF MEN—WASHINGTON

Witness more: Good and altogether proper Longfellow, coming long after Washington, could exclaim, "He who has not been at a tavern knows not what a paradise it is.—O holy tavern! O miraculous tavern!—holy, because no carking cares are there, nor weariness, nor pain; and miraculous, because of the spits."

In 1790 Washington lodges at Warne's Tavern, Jamaica, L. I.,—"a pretty good and decent house." At South Hempstead he receives welcome "at the House of one Simmons, formerly a tavern, now of private entertainment for money."

At Amityville he puts up at Zebulon Ketcham's Inn, "which had also been a public House, but now a private one—receiving pay for what it furnished—this house a very neat and decent one."

Soon he finds another, Squire Thompson's, "such a house as the last, that is, one that is not public but will receive pay for everything it furnishes, in the same manner as if it was." Does he smile here? It would seem so.

Again we find him at Hart's Tavern, in Brookhaven Township, or baiting his horses at the Widow Blidenberg's, Smith's Tavern, "a decent house fifteen miles from Huntington." Here he lodges at the Widow Platt's Tavern, "and it was tolerable good." What is *decent* is important and it goes into writing.

At King's-bridge, 1789, we find him at Caleb

CONTEMPT FOR THE POPULACE

Hyatt's Tavern, also at the Widow Haviland's Tavern at Rye—"a very neat and decent Inn." Travelling over hilly and stony roads "trying to Wheels and Carriages" he is discovered at Webb's Tavern, Stamford, "a tolerable good house."

At New Haven he writes: "The number of Souls in it are said to be about 4000. There is a College in which there are at this time 120 Students lodged at the House of Mr. Brown, who keeps a good tavern." The Yale students are merely tavern infestors. They even sleep there! Why not another book—on the wickedness of Old Yale?

Carrington's Tavern, at Wallingford, is "but an ordinary house." At Hartford he lodges at Bull's Tavern. October 21, 1790, he enters this at Windsor: "And many other Gentlemen sat an hour or two with me in the evening at Parson's Tavern, where I lodged, and which is a good House."

Again we find him in the Scott House, at Palmer, and "at the house of one Isaac Jenks, who keeps a pretty good tavern," at Spencer. So runs the Evil Day.

Always commencing his course *with the sun*, he makes it a rule to push on twelve or fourteen miles before breakfast. So Friday, October 23, 1790, we find him knocking at the doors of the United States Arms, in Worcester, for breakfast. He is fifty-eight years old.

GREATEST OF MEN—WASHINGTON

Even the houses along the way he describes.

"No dwelling house is seen without a Stone or Brick Chimney, and rarely any without a shingled roof—generally the sides are shingled also. The Destructive evidences of British cruelty are yet visible . . . as there are the Chimneys of many burned houses standing yet."

He refers to Connecticut.

Of the decency and stability of the people in Massachusetts he writes, 1789:

"There is a great equality in the People of this State. Few or no opulent men—and no poor—great similitude in their buildings . . . a Chimney always of Stone or Brick, and door in the middle, with a stair case fronting the door—two flush stories with a very good show of sash and glass windows."

Along the way: "The superb Landscape is a rich regalia. We found all the Farmers busily employed in gathering, grinding and expressing the Juice of their apples." Who is there who would not have loved this man? There have been no heroics here! No statesmanship! Just a man!

Yet he has "contempt for the populace." His keen *interest* in their houses and occupations is, of course, the best evidence of *disinterest and contempt*. He all but counts the shingles. He loves the old stone or brick chimney. He rejoices over the very good show of sash and glass windows. He frequently applies the word "decent" as a sort of poultice to his conscience. The caricature permits of no other interpretation. To know that there are no poor makes him wince. Rather would he have it otherwise. No, one can't make a cartoon of Washington without sickening at the task.

CHAPTER XXI

INCONSIDERATE, IMPERIOUS

SATURDAY, October 24, 1789, Washington is in Cambridge, where he lodges at the Widow Ingersoll's. Again he records the description: "A very decent and good house." Tuesday, October 27, at 3 o'clock, he dines at a large and elegant dinner at Faneuil Hall, spending the evening at his lodging. Two days later he leaves Boston, noting that "the bridges of Charlestown and Malden are useful and noble—doing great credit to the enterprising spirit of the people of this State."

All this is mere window-dressing for future generations to gaze at. Washington is a sort of stage manager grouping "useful and noble" properties so that they may attract the maximum attention. Did biographer ever indulge in such useless and ignoble chatter? Where, in the history of letters, has meanness been so sublimated?

During the afternoon of the 29th Washington visits the home of Mrs. Lee in Marblehead, followed by a large company who partake of a cold collation. In the evening he meets "at least an hundred handsome and well-dressed ladies," but as usual, how-

INCONSIDERATE, IMPERIOUS

ever luring the attraction, he is back at his lodging at nine o'clock.

Let it not be forgotten that it is the custom of his life to be *out of bed with the sun*. Early morning, Friday, October 30, he is on his way, passing through Salem and Beverley, across the bridge for Newbury-Port, and so on to New Hampshire, arriving at Portsmouth before three in the afternoon. There he "drank tea with a large circle of Ladies" and retired a little after seven o'clock.

Might it be impertinent to ask how frequently the modern biographer retires as early?

Wednesday, November 4, he sets out for Exeter, the second town in New Hampshire. Continuing through to Kingston his horses are pushed till he arrives at Haverhill, where he "stayed all night at Harrod's Tavern."

Thursday morning he is out of bed before sunup. Crossing the Merrimac River, he drives nine miles before breakfast, which is served at Abbot's Tavern in Andover. Thence to Lexington for dinner "and view the spot on which the first blood was spilt in the dispute with Great Britain on the 19th of April, 1775," fourteen years before.

At least he knows his history. One may retort that he should know it. No man deserves undue credit for being familiar with his own handiwork. It just as surely follows that no man unfamiliar

GREATEST OF MEN—WASHINGTON

with truth deserves credit of any kind for twisting it out of shape.

A tired Washington is difficult to picture. That he did tire is suggested by his memory of Watertown, "where we lodged at the house of Widow Coolidge, near the bridge, and a very indifferent one it is." On the way home the same tired Washington lodged at Taft's Tavern, one mile from Uxbridge, "where the entertainment was not very inviting."

November 7, 1789, the same tired Washington breakfasts at Jacobs' Tavern in Thompson, twelve miles from Taft's, "not a good house." Tired as he is, *he makes twelve miles before breakfast.* Catch a modern broker, banker, or captain of industry at such a performance. With Washington it is the rule, not the exception. No matter where he lodges he is out before sunrise and on his way, refusing to pause for breakfast until he has made ten or fifteen miles. Declining to burden the cook by getting her out of bed at an unreasonable hour, he prefers to make his early start and come to some place for his coffee, hoe cakes and honey at the usual and appointed time. "But, General, we shall be most happy to prepare your breakfast at four and shall regard the privilege an honor." "Please say no more, sir, I shall not permit it but I thank you."

Here we have the likeness of an inconsiderate,

INCONSIDERATE, IMPERIOUS

imperious, contemptible personage so swollen with pride that he not only takes advantage of host's readiness to rout out the servants in the wee small hours but insists that the whole household shall get up and be about to do him homage.

If truly we can judge a great man by the little things of his life we have so many little things by which to judge George Washington that we can afford to ignore all the big things in rescuing his fame from the slingers of wet earth.

Notice his tolerance for enacted ordinances and statutes. Sunday, November 8,

"it being contrary to law and disagreeable to the People of this State (Connecticut) to travel on the Sabbath day—and my horses, wanting rest, I stayed at Perkins' Tavern (Pomfret) which, by the bye, is not a good one, all day."

Ah, but this forbearance is for the sake of the horses. True enough, but why have we no comment of impatience, annoyance or resentment? The tavern is not a good one, but surely there is no reason for extolling virtues it lacks and much reason for expressing vexation in having to endure its squallor.

Monday he lodges at Hartford. Another sunrise, another ride, another breakfast, this time at Fuller's Inn, Worthington. Pushing on he lodges at New Haven, failing to mention the name of the tavern. But he does mention *sunrise*, Wednesday, November 11, at which hour he is off for West Haven for breakfast.

Observe his constancy. Leaving the Widow Haviland's, Friday, the 13th, "*as soon as we could see the road*," he breakfasts at Hoyet's Tavern, near King's-bridge, and so returns to New York, "where I find Mrs. Washington and the rest of the family all well—and it being Mrs. Washington's night to receive visits, a pretty large company of ladies and gentlemen were present." Simple tale, simple man, or, if you will, astounding tale, astounding man!

CHAPTER XXII

MADEIRA, PORT AND RHENISH

DURING Washington's tour of 1789 there are no more lords in America. But in 1774 the Colonies are still British. So we find him on the way to New York on horse-back. He has set out from his home, his plantations and his mill and has got as far as Burlington, N. J., where he is dining with the Governor of the Crown. Now he is at Baskingridge dining with Lord Sterling. After four days in the saddle he puts up, May 26, at Hull's Tavern, corner Thames and Broadway, where he attends a banquet given by the citizens to General Gage, commander-in-chief of the British troops in the Colonies.

He is younger by fifteen years than when we saw him last, and we are interested in his habits. Does he get up with the sun, or was this custom a later affectation? Being a frivolous flirt very much younger and capable of downing larger quantities of grog the night before it is important to observe the morning after. Is he still fresh enough to tumble out of bed, or must he lie there until headache abates sufficiently to let him crawl forth? What about that breakfast?

He has been hobnobbing with the nobility, mind you, and is now on his way home. May 31 he begins his journey. Dines at New Ark and lodges at Amboy. Before the rustics are up and about he is in the saddle. It is June 1 and the road is still in darkness, but he canters all the way to Brunswick for breakfast, lodging for the night at Bristol, Pa. June 3 we find him at the Sorrel Horse, a tavern on the old Lancaster Road, thirteen miles from Philadelphia. At night he lodges at the Ship Tavern, thirty-four miles off. He is still "drunk" enough to be out of bed with the sun on the morning of June 4, and we find him driving thirteen miles before breakfast, which he eats at the Sign of the Bull.

It's difficult to keep up with him, for he dines at Lancaster and makes no stop till he reaches Wright's Ferry, where we lodge with him until sun-up. Off we go again to get no breakfast on the morning of June 5 till we reach Yorktown. Still in the saddle we arrive at the Sign of the Buck at Haverford, where we dine. We have to make Sutton's Tavern before night, where we lodge. In the morning it's the same old story. We get no breakfast till we have "rid ten miles from Sutton's to Slade's Tavern." We pick up what we can on the way, and

MADEIRA, PORT AND RHENISH

don't eat again till we breakfast, June 7, at Widow Ramsey's Inn, fifteen miles from Baltimore Town. Lodging at Calvert's House, we get back to Mt. Vernon June 8 at two in the afternoon, marvelously fresh and sober.

The old inns and taverns have disappeared. Had their proprietors been gifted with prophetic vision they might have bequeathed to their offspring for generations to come an advertisement of compelling lure—"Here George Washington was Entertained and Lodged on Such and Such a Day and Night."

It would be quite unfair to miss any of the old taverns, so we must include the fact that October 12, 1774, Washington finds refreshment at Peg Mullen's Beef Steak House, Philadelphia. He was attending the First Continental Congress. You would never suspect the fact from any hint of it in his diary.

Ten years have passed. The war is over. Washington is travelling, September 1, 1784. He needs eight horses, three servants, and enormous baggage. His direction is westward. He lodges at Sheppar's Tavern, twenty-five miles from Philadelphia. Pushing off in the early morning of September 2, he continues until noon, dining at Roper's Tavern and lodging at Thompson's, thirty-six miles further along.

Let us see him make the mountains which are

GREATEST OF MEN—WASHINGTON

"tedious and fatiguing. From Fort Cumberland to Gwins took me one hour and ten Minutes riding—between Gwins and Tumbersons. I was near 6 hours and used all the dispatch I could—between Tumbersons and Mounts's I was full 4 hours—between Mount's and the crossing upwards of 3 hours—to Daughertys 4 hours—to Gists 4 1-4 hours—to Simpsons 3 hours and in all parts of the Road that would admit it I endeavored to ride my usual travelling gate of 5 Miles an hour."

Among the establishments affording refreshment and lodging are Evan Wynn's Tavern, Allegheny County, Pa., "at the forks of the road leading to Winchester and the old town, distant twenty miles," Tumblestone's Tavern and the Mountain Inn or White Oak Springs.

October 22, 1784, headed for Beasentown (now Uniontown, Fayette County), we are permitted to peek into Washington's baggage, consisting of two leather and one linen valises, two tents with poles, etc., bedding, an equipage trunk with silver cups, spoons, canteens, two kegs of spirits, horseshoes. Washington writes: "Note—In my equipage Trunk and the Canteens were Madeira and Port Wine, Cherry bounce, oyl, mustard, vinegar, spices of all sorts, Tea and Sugar in the camp kettles—etc."

September, 1785, he is lodged at the New Tavern

MADEIRA, PORT AND RHENISH

at Alexandria, where he engages Tom McCarthy to come home with him as his Household Steward at a wage of £30 per annum.

We might look into his purchases to be sent to Mt. Vernon. They include a case of pickles to consist of anchovies, capers, olives, oyl and India mangoes in bottles, one large Cheshire cheese, four pounds green tea, twenty-five pounds best Jar Raisins, twenty-five pounds almonds in the shell, one hogshead best porter, ten loaves double and ten single refined sugar, twelve pounds best mustard, one hundred pounds biscuit, three gallons Rhenish in bottles, twenty sacks salt, five pounds white sugar candy, ten pounds brown sugar candy, one pound barley sugar, ten shillings worth of Toys, six little books for children beginning to read, one fashionable dressed doll and other toys 20s., four pounds anniseed, four pounds cummin seed, four pounds fenegreek, two pounds licorice juice, four pounds long pepper.

What's all this about? Nothing but home: Whatsoever he puts up with in the inns, he is not unmindful of the household at Mt. Vernon.

CHAPTER XXIII

THE SPIRIT OF THE TAVERN

AS the inns and taverns have so much to tell us about Washington, that otherwise would remain unknown, to slight them in the least, however unexciting the tale they tell, would smack of ingratitude. They disclose traits of character which no biographer has ever stressed, and enable us to see their guest no farther away than across the table.

It is now 1791, and we must be off with him from Philadelphia for a tour through the south. His equipage consists of

"a Charriot and four horses drove in hand— a light baggage Waggon and two horses—four saddle horses besides a led one for myself—and five—to wit; my Valet de Chambre, two footmen, Coachmen and Postilion."

He is in his sixtieth year, but the chariot is tedious, hence the led horse for himself. He can move from chariot to saddle at will. On the way we stop at Wythe's Inn at Chester, Brindley's Inn at Wilmington, the Red Lion at Newcastle, the Buck Tavern thirteen miles distant, the Worrell

THE SPIRIT OF THE TAVERN

House at Chester, Mann's Tavern along the way, and Suter's Tavern not far from George-Town.

April 10, 1791, we dine in the Bowling Green at Todd's Ordinary, lodge at Kenner's Tavern fourteen miles farther, and then to Richmond, where Washington fails to mention his lodgings. Fifteen miles from Petersburg we breakfast, Friday, April 15, at Lee's Tavern, and after fifteen miles hard going we lodge "at the House of one Oliver, where there are tolerable clean beds."

Continuing our journey we breakfast at "Andrews', a small but decent House." Monday, April 18, we dine at Slaughter's Tavern, twenty-two miles from Halifax, and Wednesday, 20th, we find "exceeding good lodging" at the Stanley House, Newbern, on the confluence of the Rivers Neuse and Trent.

Shrine's Tavern, ten miles from Newbern, and Sage's Tavern, a good ride hence, and indifferent, but Dorsey's Tavern at Wilmington is good. Russe's Inn, twenty-five miles from Wilmington, is indifferent.

Wednesday, May 4, we dine at McCreddy's Tavern at Charlestown and at Purysburg, May 12, we find "very good lodgings" at Brown's Coffee House. Poking our way through the country, we are lodged and refreshed at Russell's Inn, Spencer's Tavern, Garnet's Tavern, Pierce's Tavern,

Spinner's Tavern, Lambert's Tavern, and Tulcher's Inn, on the road to Waynesborough, between Savannah and Augusta.

Twenty-nine miles from Augusta, May 21, we dine at the Piney Woods House. May 30, having breakfasted at Yarborough's Tavern, we move on to Salisbury, where the citizens have prepared a public dinner at Hughes' Hotel for their idol. June 1 we are lodged at the old Salem Tavern at Salem, "a small but neat village." From Petersburg to Halifax Old Town the houses along the road "are altogether of Wood and chiefly of logs—some indeed have brick chimneys but generally the chimneys are of split sticks filled with dirt between them. The Houses, though not elegant, are in general decent from Staunton to Charlotte Ct. Ho., and bespeak good livers; being for the most part weather-boarded and shingled with brick Chimneys."

June 8 we lodge at Moore's Tavern, two miles from Carter's Ferry over James River. June 30 we dine at Peter's Tavern, twenty miles from Williamsburg, sixteen miles from Washington. At Fredericktown we lodge at Brothers Tavern. September 30 we spend the night at the Trappe Tavern on the old Germantown Road, twenty-five miles from Philadelphia.

Save only for a note here and there that the entertainment afforded is indifferent, Washington

THE SPIRIT OF THE TAVERN

complains neither of food nor lodging. On the other hand he never fails to emphasize the significance of qualities he loves to assemble under the word "decent."

To understand the sentiment of the times toward the taverns we must realize that from the year 1700 they had become the very cradles of liberty in the Colonies. The Black Horse Tavern, 1727, by direction of the Assembly, became the meeting place of the Committee on Grievances every Tuesday and Friday, and so continued for years. At the Black Horse, 1735, was celebrated the victory of the colonists in maintaining the rights of free speech and the liberty of the press, won by Andrew Hamilton, a Philadelphia lawyer, in his defense of John Peter Zenger. That gentleman's bitter attacks against official abuses so drove the governor to frenzy that he clapped him in jail and demanded that he be burned by the common hangman. The grand jury refused to indict, but the prisoner was nevertheless kept in jail, where he continued to edit the New York Weekly Journal through a hole in his cell until finally released through Hamilton's amazing eloquence.

W. Harrison Bayles asserts that if the Black Horse Tavern was not the cradle of liberty it was certainly the nursery of those sentiments which ripened into the Declaration of Independence.

GREATEST OF MEN—WASHINGTON

Many of these old establishments were resplendent with elegance. As early as January 19, 1736,

"a most magnificent Appearance of gentlemen and ladies celebrated His Royal Highness's birthday at the Black Horse, New York, with a grand ball, French and country dances, a most sumptuous entertainment conducted with the utmost Decency, Mirth and Cheerfulness."

In 1769 Vauxhall Gardens, frequented by Washington, opened for the

"Reception of Ladies and Gentlemen, illuminated every evening in the Week; Coffee, Tea and Hot Rolls, neat Wines and other Liquors with Cakes—a Concert of Music, Vocal and Instrumental—Dinners or Suppers dressed in a most Elegant Manner."

In 1775 Edward Bardin opened the Corner House in the Fields. The cloth was laid "With Roast Beef, Veal, Mutton, Lamb, Ducks and Chickens, Gammon, Lobsters, Pickled Oysters, Custards, Tarts, Chicken Pies, Tea and Coffee."

No, the inns and taverns were not low places and no effort to interpret Washington's frequent mention of them as evidence of his "careless and roistering life" can end in anything but falsehood and calumny.

CHAPTER XXIV

PAID FOR IN MONEY

ONE of the big little hours of Washington's life can be fixed in the morning of December 4, 1783, when he meets with his officers at Fraunces' Tavern. They are never to meet again as soldiers. The occasion is the farewell of the commander-in-chief to the generals and colonels who stood by him through the Revolution. Let us look on. The scene bears repetition.

As Washington enters the room on the Broad Street side he cannot conceal his emotions. He had just written to Lafayette:

"We are now an independent people, and have yet to learn political tactics. We are placed among the nations of the earth and have a character to establish. How we shall acquit ourselves time must discover. The probability is, at least I fear it, that local politics will interfere too much with the more liberal and extensive plan of government which wisdom and foresight free from prejudice would dictate, and that we shall be guilty of many blunders before we shall have arrived at any perfection. Experience purchased at the price of difficulties and distress will alone convince us that the honor, power

GREATEST OF MEN—WASHINGTON

and true interest of this country must be measured by a Continental scale and that every departure therefrom must weaken the Union and may ultimately break the band which holds us together. To avert these evils, to form a new constitution, that will give consistency, stability and dignity to the Union, and sufficient powers to the great council of the nation for general purposes, is a duty incumbent upon every man who wishes well to his country, and will meet with my aid as far as it can be rendered in the private walks of life."

It is a grave hour, and to have to say goodby to his companions in arms, bound to him by ties of feeling never to be adequately described, is so deeply moving that only silence can lend its aid to the trial.

Washington can scarcely speak. His voice is broken. He fills a glass. The tension snaps. Then these few words: "With a heart full of love and gratitude I take leave of you. I most devoutly wish that your latter days may be as prosperous and happy as your former ones have been glorious and honorable. I cannot come to each of you to take my leave but shall be obliged if each of you will come and take me by the hand."

General Knox is nearest. Washington, unable to speak further, embraces him. They all come forward. Not another word. The manliness of the tears in every eye is womanly. The womanly tenderness of the unutterable emotions aroused in every

PAID FOR IN MONEY

breast is manly. Such mute and solemn scenes are not often witnessed in this world.

The long siege is over. The Tories and lovers of the Crown have made it hard and bitter. The faithful ones who for themselves had all to lose and little to gain except for their fellows, are in the group perhaps never to be assembled again.

Washington's outward appearance of reserve, usually like that of marble, has melted under the burning fire of sentiment and affection which flames in his heart.

His forty-four brave, devoted and noble companions include in addition to General Knox, Greene, Gates, Kosciusko, Carroll, Steuben, Wayne, Lincoln, Lee, Moultry, Putnam, Stark, Hamilton, Colonels Humphreys, Fish, Talmadge and Governor Clinton. Taverns were Things that lived!

All leave the room, and passing out through a corps of light infantry walk to White Hall, where a barge is waiting to convey the General to Paulus Hook. The whole company "with dejected countenances, testifying feelings of delicious melancholy," stand by as Washington enters the barge. Turning to them he waves his hat but does not speak. He cannot.

Congress has adjourned from Princeton to Annapolis. There Washington resigns his commission and takes his leave of all the employments of public life.

GREATEST OF MEN—WASHINGTON

The next morning, December 23, he reaches Mt. Vernon.

Except for the single accident that enabled him while on his march to Count Rochambeau at Yorktown to pause briefly at his own house, he had been absent from that loved abode, in command of the army, more than eight years and a half. Who is the American who will now *give* as much to the saving of America?

His private affairs have been deranged by the disorders of the time and his inability to give them his personal attention. The Supreme Executive Council of Pennsylvania, because "his illustrious actions and virtues render his character so splendid and venerable" undertakes to compensate him for his public services. "We are perfectly acquainted with the disinterestedness and generosity of his soul. He thinks himself amply rewarded for all his labors and cares, by the love and prosperity of his fellow-citizens. It is true, no rewards they can bestow can be equal to his merits. But they ought not to suffer those merits to be burdensome to him."

So Washington is to be paid in money. "We are aware of the delicacy with which this subject must be treated." Quite obviously the Supreme Executive Council have given considerable thought to their project.

But they haven't reckoned with Washington, and

PAID FOR IN MONEY

the moment he hears of the movement he stops the proceedings and Congress is not permitted ever to address itself to the subject. What Washington *gave* was given! Love and service were not commodities of trade to be bartered for cash.

This is the man who in his will provides for the freedom of his slaves upon the death of his wife. To emancipate them at once

"though earnestly wished by me, would be attended with such insuperable difficulties, on account of their intermixture by marriage with the dower Negroes, as to excite the most painful sensations, if not disagreeable consequences to the latter, it not being in my power, under the tenure by which the dower Negroes are held, to manumit them."

So among those who, receiving their freedom, "will be unable to support themselves because of old age or bodily infirmities or on account of their infancy" he provides that they shall be comfortably clothed and fed as long as they live.

To William he gives immediate freedom with an annuity of thirty dollars during his natural life independent of the victuals and clothes he has been accustomed to receive.

And they tell us Washington was a hard man, a calculating man, a grasping man, a business man, a dull man, a passionate man, an altogether common man, a mere Human Animal.

CHAPTER XXV

THE COLD AND SILENT MAN

DID all his knocking-about combined with the hardships of war chill the affections of Washington's nature? We haven't finished with him at the inns, but surely such haphazard accommodations as they afforded and such manners as they tended to engender might have had some influence upon the hardening of his character. That he was a hard character you have been violently informed. Let us peep over his shoulder as he sits at his writing table at Mt. Vernon, November 25, 1784. He is merely dropping a line to the little daughter of Papa Lafayette across the sea. Will the letter be gracious, gentle, even beautiful? To follow his pen is easy.

"Permit me to thank my dear little correspondent for the favor of her letter of the 18th of June last, and to impress her with the idea of the pleasure I shall derive from a continuance of them. Her papa is restored to her with all the good health, paternal affection, and honors, which her tender heart could wish. He will carry a kiss to her from me which might be more agreeable from a pretty boy, and give

THE COLD AND SILENT MAN

her assurances of the affectionate regard with which I have the pleasure of being her well-wisher."

Washington had written the child's dear mother in most unrestrained terms of his love for her and her little George and Virginia,

"whose names do honor to my country and to myself. Freed from the clangor of arms and the bustle of a camp, from the cares of public employment and the responsibility of office, I am now enjoying domestic ease under the shadow of my own vine and my own fig-tree; and in a small villa, with the implements of husbandry and lambkins around me, I expect to glide gently down the stream of life, till I am entombed in the mansion of my fathers."

So he goes on talking of Martha, who "is too much immersed in the care of her little progeny, (the four children of her deceased son John Parke Custis) to cross the Atlantic."

Without Martha he will not journey to France. That the French would make a god of him he knows. He has no desire to be a god, so he begs the wife of Lafayette to come to Mt. Vernon for she

"must have a curiosity to see the country, young, rude, and uncultivated as it is, for the liberties of which your husband has fought, bled, and acquired much glory, where everybody admires, everybody loves him. Come, then, let me entreat you and call my cottage your home; for your own doors do not open to you with more readiness than mine would. You will see the plain manner in which we live, and meet with rustic civility; and you shall taste the simplicity of rural life. It will diversify the scene, and may give you a higher relish for the gaieties of the court when you return to Versailles."

The lady does not come, so Washington again writes her, May 10, 1786, begging her to come so that he and Martha may have an opportunity of expressing to her personally those sentiments of attachment and love with which she has inspired them. She must bring the children to honor the young folks of his own family, to cement the friendship which seems to be rising in their tender breasts, to increase the flames of it which they have imbibed from the conversation of the household, flames to which nothing can add strength but the endearments that flow from personal interviews and the unrestrained exchange of liberal sentiment.

"Will you not, then, madam, afford them this oportunity? May we hope for it soon. The noontide of life is now past with Mrs. Washington and myself; and all we have to do is to spend the evening of our days in tranquility. We must forego the pleasure of visiting you, but the case with you is far otherwise. In the natural order of things you have many years to come. My mother will

THE COLD AND SILENT MAN

receive the compliments you honor her with, as flattering marks of attention, and I shall have great pleasure in delivering them myself."

These surely were the sentiments of a mountebank of hard and cruel nature, of a gambler at cards, a wine-bibber and a profligate. There is no poetry in them, no impulse of gratitude, no love of children, wife, or home. The inns and taverns of his day had blunted Washington's sensibilities. His gaming at cards had dulled all the finer qualities of his nature. His prodigious swearing had coarsened his speech.

The combination of gross self-indulgence and uncurbed dissipations had blotted all delicacy from his heart. These tender and feeling letters must either be pure fictions or unscrupulous inventions designed to defend the reputation of as brave and gallant a soul as ever animated human flesh, a reputation that should need no defense.

What have we come to, with our scalpels so sharp, our acids so biting, our malice so corrosive that we must fall upon the one man who for sheer nobility must ever be, as he deserves to be, a model to the youth of the nation he brought into existence? Have we acquired some new malignant disease that would inspire us to kill the bodies of living men were it not for cowardice, and must therefore con-

GREATEST OF MEN—WASHINGTON

tent ourselves with destroying the reputation of the dead who cannot rise to repel assault?

Who is there who can honestly read Washington's private letters and public papers without bending his knee in reverence? Who is there who can honestly read his diary without loving him for what he was? If ever man merited immortality Washington is with God.

CHAPTER XXVI

AN EPIC OF HATRED

THE graciousness of Washington is not confined to little children or to those he loves. Even his most hateful enemies, who seek to destroy him, stir no desire of revenge in his heart. Each new evidence of ingratitude, perfidy and treachery brings him sorrow but no disturbance of his poise.

Not even Gates or Mifflin or Conway in all their painful intrigues can arouse him to revenge. The spurious pamphlets published in London, 1776, designed to reveal him as a Thing of Evil, fail to excite his indignation. Their subsequent publication in America leaves him unmoved.

The anonymous letters sent to the president of Congress and the governor of Virginia, filled with insinuations and falsehoods designed to destroy him, evoke no more than a letter to President Laurens:

"My enemies take an ungenerous advantage of me. They know the delicacy of my situation, and that motives of policy deprive me of the defense I might otherwise make against their insidious attacks. They know I cannot combat their insinuations, however injurious, without disclosing secrets,

GREATEST OF MEN—WASHINGTON

which it is of the utmost moment to conceal. But why should I expect to be exempt from censure, the unfailing lot of an elevated station? Merit and talents, with which I can have no pretensions of rivalship, have ever been subject to it. My heart tells me, that it has been my unremitted aim to do the best that circumstances would permit; yet I may have been very often mistaken in my judgment of the means, and may in many instances deserve the imputations of error."

Do ordinary men respond thus to undeserved assault? This indeed is nobility exalted! Yet the wickedness and the horror of the activities aimed at Washington's heart were so profoundly moving that Lafayette had best testify: "I see plainly that America can defend herself, but I begin to fear that she may be lost by herself and her own sons."

Lafayette knows Washington; Washington knows Lafayette. Years later the noblest American who ever lived embraced and kissed this noble son of France. Happily we possess Lafayette's picture of Washington, through his letter to Baron Steuben, March 12, 1778—a picture that grew even warmer in its color as the years went on.

"Permit me," writes Lafayette, "to express my satisfaction at your having seen General Washington. No enemies to that great man can be found, except among the enemies to his country; nor is it

AN EPIC OF HATRED

possible for any man of a noble spirit to refrain from loving the excellent qualities of his heart. His honesty, his frankness, his sensibility, his virtue to the full extent in which this word can be understood, are above all praise. It is not for me to judge of his military talents, but his advice in council has always appeared to me the best, although his modesty prevents him sometimes from sustaining it; and his predictions have generally been fulfilled. I am the more happy in giving you this opinion of my friend, with all the sincerity which I feel, because some persons may perhaps attempt to deceive you."

Even poor Conway, who sold himself to Washington's enemies and whose wretched intrigues resulted in a duel and a grievous wound, believing himself to be dying, wrote to Washington:

"My career will soon be over, therefore justice and truth prompt me to declare my last sentiments. You are in my eyes the great and good man. May you long enjoy the love, veneration and esteem of these States, whose liberties you have asserted by your virtues."

This tribute from an enemy, issuing from a solemn hour, offsets the enthusiasm of the generous friend and becomes all the more eloquent by reason of the dictates of conscience which provoke such belated expression of the inmost feelings of a tor-

GREATEST OF MEN—WASHINGTON

tured soul. Do men, not truly great, so inspire the love and veneration of their enemies?

But is Washington, so well beloved by friend and enemy, beloved by his own wife? The meanest insinuations have focused on this issue. What sentiments, therefore, does he actually inspire in the heart of Mrs. Washington? The famine at Valley Forge is real. There are but blankets enough for half the starving men. Yet in the very midst of winter Mrs. Washington leaves the comforts of her home, and joins her husband at Valley Forge. Washington is in his forty-fifth year. His wife, of the same age, wants to be near him. You have already seen that she wanted to share the war with him, away from Mt. Vernon and actually did share with him all the hardships of *all* his Winter Quarters throughout the struggle.

It is now 1789. Washington is fifty-seven. Mrs. Washington is writing to Mrs. Warren.

"I little thought," she says, "when the war was finished, that any circumstances could possibly happen which would call the General into public life again. I had anticipated, that from that moment we should be suffered to grow old together in solitude and tranquility. That was the first and dearest wish of my heart. His feelings and my own were in perfect unison with respect to our predilection for private life. The consciousness of having at-

AN EPIC OF HATRED

tempted to do all the good in his power, and the pleasure of finding his fellow citizens so well satisfied with the disinterestedness of his conduct, will doubtless be some compensation for the great sacrifices which I know he has made."

Married on the sixth of January, 1759, three months younger than himself, or eight months older, according to some computations, this woman had lived with her husband thirty years when she wrote that the first and dearest wish of her heart had ever been that he and she might be suffered to grow old together in solitude and tranquillity.

Friend, enemy and wife tell the same story.

But in the meantime the enthusiasm of the populace for his person has become so great that he cannot move in any direction

"without drawing around him thousands of spectators eager to gratify their eyes, to greet him with acclamations of joy, and to exhibit testimony of their veneration. Men, women and children, people of all ranks, ages and occupations, assemble from far and near at the crossings of the roads and other places where it was known he would pass."

As priests are men, not angels, so was Washington man, not saint. But such a man! Strip him bare, carve him up, autopsy him. All the fictions, poor things they were, are vanishing. White light beats down upon him. This you find. He did love truth. He did venerate justice and honesty. He did forgive every form of human weakness. He did break out in anger only to check himself upon the instant. He did kneel at Valley Forge precisely as he knelt years before at the bedside of little Patcy Custis.

As son, brother, husband and foster-father he was loving and devoted. There was no envy in him, no futile pride, no petty vanity, no reckless ambition. His great passion was love of country, love of duty, love of home. Loving his neighbor as himself, he fulfilled in spirit as in letter the highest of all laws. I make no claim to inspiration and therefore must hazard as mere opinion the deep and joyous conviction that as Washington gave all he had to the greatest experiment in liberty and independence the world has ever known, when the world was sick unto death for the very need of liberty, and as in the natural order he possessed the very gifts of mind and soul necessary to the accomplishment of his well-nigh hopeless and impossible undertaking, God raised him to the task!

CHAPTER XXVII

WASHINGTON'S ILLITERACY

MUCH is made by the 1926 biographers of Washington's "illiteracy." He never would have read at all if Sally Fairfax hadn't induced him to devote himself to a few books. He did indeed read part of the Spectator. Beyond this there is no evidence that he ever read anything. In fact he confesses that he can't read.

The violent contempt of truth set forth in this premise and the astounding conclusions based upon it are quite as valuable when viewed as history as any of the other distortions and mutilations preceding or following them.

Washington had a remarkable library. What a pity the 1926 biographers have not examined the books he read. It was so easy to discover them. They have all been preserved in the Boston Athenæum. We have a "Catalogue of the Washington Collection" by Appleton P. C. Griffin, with notes by Washington himself.

True indeed is the fact that during his later years he was denied leisure and had no opportunity whatsoever to take a book from its shelf. He even com-

GREATEST OF MEN—WASHINGTON

plains of this. Following his second term as president he was not permitted to remain a private citizen reposing at Mt. Vernon "amidst all its endearments." Within the year we find him summoned again by his country to her service.

The elder Adams is president. He tells the country what he wants and the country responds with one voice. Nothing will suit him and nothing will suit the country but Washington's acceptance of the supreme command of the army during the difficulties that have broken out between America and her old ally, France. Reluctantly Washington accepts, but on condition that he shall receive no pay or emolument of any kind until actually called into the field.

Yet even this conditional acceptance heaps new burdens upon his back, exposing him "to many official calls, to a heavy correspondence, and to a flow of company."

These are his own words, and so he writes to his ever-affectionate and ever-faithful secretary, Tobias Lear. He laments that these new fresh duties are hindrances against the putting of his private affairs in that order so necessary before he embarks in new scenes.

How can any American forget that from 1775 to 1799, a period of twenty-four years, all Washington's time was absorbed in public service? We

WASHINGTON'S ILLITERACY

know how his heart yearned for Mt. Vernon, because during the presidency alone he actually made fifteen trips to the old mansion. It may be said these trips were necessary because Washington's estate was not being properly managed. It had been neglected so long that his plantations were no longer self-supporting, and his embarrassments for ready money were frequently so severe that he often wondered to what or to whom he might turn for at least temporary relief.

He was land poor. His "people," as he called his slaves, had to be fed and clothed. He would have no blankets for them but the best. Yes, this is plain fact as his very specific and technical correspondence with the manager of his estate reveals.

Mrs. Washington had to have ready money. He instructs Tobias Lear to see that she receives all she needs and not to wait until she asks, because she is reluctant to ask, but to break in upon her from time to time and make sure that she is not embarrassed.

The people won't let him rest. The stream of enthusiasts and idly-curious pouring in upon Mt. Vernon is never interrupted. Privacy has fled forever. Self-seekers storm his gates. His home has become a shrine of patriotism and a clearing-house of petitions. He can scarcely digest the mass of letters delivered to him by every post. The special messages overwhelm him.

GREATEST OF MEN—WASHINGTON

Time to read? No wonder he himself declares that he has no time to read. The wonder is that under the circumstances anybody living in 1926 could take such words out of his own mouth and fling them back at him contemptuously. The facts of the case are so clear and forceful, so free from controversy, that to stoop to any garbling of them in an effort to destroy an idol is little short of sacrilege. Such conduct reveals a passion for falsehood, an utter disregard of the rights of the dead and the responsibilities of the living.

Not only did Washington read, but the vocabulary he acquired from his reading, *on a farm*, was so elegant and expressive that scarcely a man now living can be found to match his mastery of words. That he wrote with ease is not contradicted by his frequent deletions, interlineations and corrections. That his spelling was as careless as Abraham Lincoln's may indeed be a fact, but the words misspelled in his diary are usually the monosyllables. Moreover his diary was not intended for other eyes than his own, and his abbreviations (wch. for "which," y for "the," etc.) may well be regarded as a step toward shorthand.

Upon such slippery ground they attack him. Yet all they say or ever will be able to say serves only to exalt his greatness and to separate him so far from his assailants that men who know him

WASHINGTON'S ILLITERACY

can but yearn for the return of his like to this cynical, selfish and materialistic world.

How we need George Washington at this hour of public and private dishonesty, hypocrisy, smugness, filth, selfishness and scandal! Tear him out of the hearts of the young indeed! Would that we could put him, just as he was, into the soul of every American youth!

The trouble with the 1926 biographers is that they have not read what Washington read, and they have not read what Washington wrote.

Like grasshoppers they leap about among his pages seeking phrases, detached fragments, broken sentences, wretched hearsay, sentimental drivel, to find a text on which to hang their best sellers. When they are dead and forgotten Washington will be but coming into his own, for as time goes on the figure of this giant will assume ever larger proportions and the light shining from his countenance will be still more glorious than the faint reflection caught by Gilbert Stuart and Houdon.

CHAPTER XXVIII

THE MARY PHILIPSE SCANDAL

IN dealing with the Mary Philipse-George Washington scandal we are not seeking to destroy a legend that once was pretty, but rather to demonstrate the utter impossibility of the defamatory fiction under which Washington is pictured as a "land-hungry adventurer."

The 1926 version of the episode, published as further evidence of Washington's baseness, stresses the point that the Indians are scalping and burning everywhere. Washington's duty is in Boston. He is supposed to be a defender of the frontier family and should be engaged in military service. Instead, forgetful of his responsibility, sleeping as it were at his post, he tarries in New York. Mary Philipse of Yonkers is the cause. Young Washington, an exquisitely toileted fop, given over to gambling and scheming, will marry Mary Philipse's share of 51,102 acres. He is not in love with Mary, but he is terribly in love with her real estate.

So at last the Mary Philipse fiction must go. The historical facts are simple enough. The meet-

THE MARY PHILIPSE SCANDAL

ing between Washington and Mary was never questioned. It occurred just as surely as did Washington's meeting with Cornwallis. But the confusion incidental to the meeting has served merely the purpose of a smoke-screen to enable a 1926 biographer to attack the father of his country.

Of course it will be said, as it has been said, that Washington Irving testified to the truth of the Philipse Manor House romance. At the Philipse Manor House sentimental pilgrims are shown the very window-seat where George held Mary's hand. But it will not do to say that Washington Irving accepts the romance. He states very clearly that he does not believe the story. His words are: "That he (Washington) sought her hand but was refused is traditional and not very probable."

Nor will it do to show us the window-seat. Young Washington on his way to the Massachusetts Assembly at Boston stopped not at Yonkers, the home of Mary Philipse, but at the New York home of his old friend Beverley Robinson, the husband of a niece of Adolphus Philipse. Young Robinson and his wife give a house party and as a guest of Robinson, Washington meets Mary. Of course he admires her. Everybody does.

But however violent the admiration, Washington proceeds immediately to Boston, where he spends ten days attending the meetings of the Massachu-

GREATEST OF MEN—WASHINGTON

setts Legislature. Here expresses reach him from Winchester bringing word that the French, aided by the Indians, are making another attack upon the western settlers and from Fort Duquesne are spreading terror and desolation throughout the country.

A letter from a would-be match-maker, perhaps playfully written, urges Washington to hasten back to New York as Captain Roger Morris is storming the heart of Miss Philipse. Now what does Washington Irving say? Merely this:

"In this moment of exigency all softer claims were forgotten. Washington repaired in all haste to his post at Winchester and Captain Morris was left to urge his suit unrivalled and carry off the prize."

When did all this occur, and how much time did Washington give to his acquaintance with Mary Philipse? History deals honorably with the event, but insists that the scene shall be laid not at the Philipse Manor House in Yonkers, but at the Beverley Robinson house in New York. So we flare back to the beginning. Washington has not yet met Mary Philipse. It is February 4, 1756. He begins the horse-back journey that leads to the meeting. Riding eleven days he reaches New York, February 15. The year is 1756. We must remember this because not until two years later, January

THE MARY PHILIPSE SCANDAL

28, 1758, does Mary Philipse marry her English captain.

Whether Washington, after meeting Mary, pauses three full days or a little less we do not yet know. A little later we shall. Much business is to be done in New York and the youthful colonel can't spend the entire time with Mary, at a house party, though the assumption is that he spends much time with her and really becomes acquainted. There is another assumption. Beverley Robinson, who has married into the Philipse family, but has been so short-sighted as not to marry the Philipse heiress, must be mercenary indeed. He must have seized upon the first moment of Washington's arrival to do some whispering. Perhaps these were his very words:

"I am bringing Mary Philipse to the house. Some day she will be very rich in her own name. There's a fortune in your grasp. I will help fix things for you. Marry her. In consideration of this suggestion and my helpfulness in bringing it to a head I shall expect an adequate reward. When you get a good firm clutch upon her acres I shall be satisfied with a round commission."

How else shall we account for the extraordinary speed of Washington's activities?

At any rate Washington has some good part of

GREATEST OF MEN—WASHINGTON

three full days in which to develop the conspiracy. We know that he sets off for Boston. It is midwinter. The horse-back journey means six days' hard riding. To this we add ten days in the Massachusetts Legislature. Now comes the alarm. Washington is summoned to instantaneous action. Williamsburg, Virginia, is distant by fifteen days hard travelling. The roads are atrocious. Horses are not machines. Desperate rider that he is, he cannot make his customary fifty miles a day. Nevertheless in the third week of March he rides into Williamsburg and attends the opening of the House of Burgesses, frantically occupied with measures for the protection of the border. Fort Duquesne must be captured. Washington is aflame to undertake the work.

So we have six days from New York to Boston, ten days in Boston, sixteen days from Boston to Williamsburg, a total of thirty-two days. Flaring back from March 21, 1756, we come to February 18, the only day of Washington's departure from Mary Philipse to Boston that would enable him to keep his later schedule. Between February 15 and February 18 are three days. But Washington arrived in the evening of February 15 and departed on the morning of February 18. So we have two days to deal with. It was during these two days that he engineered his scheme of marrying Mary's acres.

THE MARY PHILIPSE SCANDAL

The New York *Mercury* of February 16 recorded his arrival on the 15th. The same paper recorded on the 26th his departure for Boston on the "Friday previous." Schroeder-Lossing miraculously fixes the "Friday previous" as February 25 and says he was in Boston, February 27—a distance by horseback of more than 250 miles. The only conclusion is that Washington exhausted six horses along the way, dismounting neither for food nor sleep. If so, there never was such a ride in the history of the world. Alas, we must go back to February 18, and stay there.

Three days, if you will, but two days actually. No wonder Washington doesn't know how to spell Mary's name. An indignant librarian retorts that this misspelling means nothing as Washington was a notoriously bad speller. Now John C. Fitzpatrick, who for many years has had charge of the Washington manuscripts in the Library of Congress, has edited the diaries from 1748 to 1799. He forgets to index "Dubourg" and leaves in doubt the place of residence of Washington's two nephews at Georgetown College. But in his preface to the diaries, published for the Mt. Vernon Ladies Association of the Union, for whose fine spirit all America should be grateful, he does not forget to say this: "It may be noted also that in the matter of spelling, a point so often dwelt upon, Washington's weakness lay in the simple words; oddly enough the difficult ones are usually spelled correctly." Fitzpatrick is an unchallengeable authority. He has lived for years with words written in Washington's own hand. So perishes another of the Washington libels heretofore accepted even by the learned deans and presidents of academies and universities.

It has been my privilege to examine more than a hundred Washington letters in the original without the discovery of a misspelled word.

But spelling has nothing to do with romance or land-grabbing. It is now many years later, 1781. Washington is conquering the enemy. Consecrated by destiny he soon will be the greatest man America has ever known. He will make possible the exhibition of Lincoln's greatness. Without him Lincoln will remain a careful, competent, marvelously balanced country lawyer. But spelling is the theme. In all his alleged familiarity with Mary Philipse he has been so strangely unheedful, so unromantically unparticular, so indifferently careless as to be still ignorant of the spelling of her name. He knows all about leases, land grants and deeds, but such very important land-grabbing and deedful spelling as "Philipse" could never get fixed in his mind.

August 6, 1781, while reconnoitering the country now known as the flats of Yonkers, Oak Hill, Park

THE MARY PHILIPSE SCANDAL

Hill, Rumsey Road, the Hudson River Country Club, the Samuel Untermeyer Estate, the Grassy Sprain Golf Club, the St. Andrew Golf Club, the Tuckahoe Road and the Philipse Manor House, he misspells the name not once, but twice.

While riding over the very spot where now stands the Thompson Institute for Plant Research, lying between the first tee and the second green, housing secrets that would have thrilled him to the soul, he was either a cold, calculating, grossly mercenary adventurer with designs upon a young woman whose riches rather than whose beauty and charm made her an object not of his love, but of his greed—either this or not this. If we cling to the sentimental, non-historical fancy we sustain the scandal-monger. If we establish a historical fact stripped of all embellishment we let the pretty fancy go by the board, and with it the scandal.

One derives no great joy in spoiling a pretty story, but a truth bearing hard upon Washington's character is greater than all the pretty stories ever written, and much more important than a pretty story employed to defame the greatest of men.

True enough the Yonkers *Statesman* resents the last moments of the legend. The Yonkers *Herald* rejoices at the demise of a tale that died from sheer inability to live beyond its allotted time.

CHAPTER XXIX

VANITY AND BIGOTRY

WHAT did the vainglorious Washington think about his own birthday? Not until two years before his death, February 22, 1797, did he ever mention it in his diary, and then only as one mentions rain in the night, or a cloudy afternoon, or an east wind—casually, indifferently.

Is it possible that all his diary entries for February 22 are blank with respect to his birthday prior to the year 1797? Such is the fact.

But because he was born February 11 under the old calendar, and because the Virginians hated the Pope, and because it was Pope Gregory who shifted Washington's birthday from February 11 to February 22, perhaps he insisted on February 11, and the record of his celebrations will be found there.

Again we are amazed by our discovery. He didn't care when his birthday was celebrated, and the only three references he makes to his birthday all occur on different days. In 1797, with the mercury at 38, we get the first mention of his "birthnight" February 22. The following year the citizens of Alexandria celebrated his birthday February

VANITY AND BIGOTRY

12, because the 11th fell on the Sabbath. They would have neither the Sabbath nor the Pope mixed up in their celebrations, so George, without protest, went with the family to the ball in his honor the year before his death. In 1799, the last of his birthdays, and the third mentioned by him, was celebrated February 11 in Alexandria, but February 22 throughout the other States.

In 1760, whether you take the 11th or the 22d, he was helping his people move a house 250 yards over ground soft and deep, with twenty hands, eight horses and six oxen, or laying in part the worm of a fence round his peach orchard. In 1768 he spent the day working on his goose pen, and at clearing the field on the creek in the neck. In 1769 he went ducking till dinner and was at court at Alexandria, but home in the evening.

In 1770 his own family, free from bigotry, were satisfied with a little surprise party to be celebrated February 22, not February 11. When he got home from court at Alexandria he found ready to greet him his brothers Samuel and John, with John's wife and daughter, also Lawrence Washington and daughter, and the Reverend Mr. Smith. Even so he fails to mention that they came to celebrate his birthday. He doesn't mention "birth day."

But, he does mention the Reverend Mr. Smith. He is always mentioning Reverend Mr. Somebody.

GREATEST OF MEN—WASHINGTON

He loves to have these men of the cloth about him. Obviously they are earnest men, sincere men, good men. Obviously there are few Elmer Gantrys among them. If Washington is clear on any subject his transparency on the subject of hypocrisy is water-white. He hates few things but he does hate deceit, sham and pose. That the clergy of his day were not dissolute, were not vicious, as charged by his 1926 libellers, is fully proved by his own respect and friendship for them. Back to his birthdays.

In 1771 he rode to his mill in the forenoon. Dr. Rumney came in the afternoon and stayed all night.

He was much fatigued by the deepness and toughness of the snow in 1772, on the 11th. On the 22d Mr. Ramsey and Capt. Conway dropped in and dined with him and stayed all night. In 1773 he "found a fox in the same place again" on the 11th, and on the 22d he stayed at home all day alone. The same thing happened in 1774. In 1775 he went ahunting, but killed nothing, on the 11th. On the 22d he went out with Mrs. Washington to Mr. Digges and dined there. Perhaps it was a birthday invitation. We shall never know.

In 1785, on the 11th, the great man was employed all day in marking the ground for the reception of his shrubs, and on the 22d he devoted himself to transplanting lilacs, mock oranges, sassa-

VANITY AND BIGOTRY

fras, dogwood and red bud. How he must have loved George Washington's birthday!

February 11, 1786, he spent the whole day in transplanting trees, principally cherry trees. February 21 a party of house guests stayed all night, but forgetful that the 22d was his birthday, they left after breakfast. Apparently he failed to remind them that a great general was going to have a birthday right there on the spot.

In 1787 he was riding over three of his plantations on horseback. On his return home he found Mr. Bryan Fairfax, his wife and daughter. In 1788 he remained at home all day.

When president, February 22, 1790, he went out on horse-back into the country to make an inspection of a new threshing machine invented by Baron de Poellnitz, thus becoming the sponsor, through his interest in agricultural machinery, of our modern Experiment Stations. "Many and respectable visitors to Mrs. Washington" came in the evening. There was no birthday even then, and no desire for one. The people who came avisiting did not offend him by their forgetfulness that upon that day a great man had been born into the world and had a right to insist that his neighbors should remember the event. Mrs. Washington received the attention, *not her husband.*

All the years not mentioned here are blanks. So

GREATEST OF MEN—WASHINGTON

we come to February 22, 1797. Washington writes: "Rain in the Night. Cloudy forenoon with the Wind at East, afterwards at S. W. Clear and very fine, went in the evening to an elegant entermt. given on my birth-night. Mercury 38."

If it were not for *Claypoole's American Daily Advertiser* we would never know that this celebration "for Splendor, Taste and Elegance, was, perhaps, never excelled by any similar entertainment in the United States."

And this is the man who was all egotist. One of the 1926 biographers tortures himself to create a circumstantial case that will reveal Washington in the light of a pope-baiter. England knew that the calendar was all wrong, and although Pope Gregory had fixed it in 1582, the English refused to accept the correction until 1752. In America the situation was worse, as opposition to the well-known sun, moon and stars could testify. Even President Ezra Stiles of Yale insisted on February 11 as late as 1779.

So the poor biographers say, "and to his dying day he thought of himself as born on February eleventh." To prove this they add: "In the last two Februarys of his life he wrote in his diary under February 11 that he "went up to Alexandria to an elegant ball and supper, etc."

The trifling character of these distortions and

VANITY AND BIGOTRY

strainings is stressed by Washington's very first recorded mention of his birthday. He fixes it himself, in his own hand, February 22, 1797, two years before his death. To say, therefore, that "to his dying day he thought of himself as born on February 11" serves merely to emphasize the wretchedness and misery of spirit in which a belittling biography can be conceived.

In matters of principle Washington was firm as the rock; in matters of taste he could drift with the tide. The good souls of Alexandria wished to do him honor on the eleventh. He would not spoil their plans by interpolating an essay on astronomy. He would go among them and receive the affection they yearned to bestow regardless of their hatred of the Pope.

Did he not journey up to Georgetown Catholic College, March 15, 1797, where the Pope in political matters was a nonentity but in matters of faith and morals the very antithesis of the Alexandria effigy?

Did he not, July 10, 1798, entertain at dinner at Mt. Vernon the Catholic priest, Father Dubourg, then president of Georgetown, afterwards bishop of New Orleans, together with another of the Catholic professors and two of the Catholic students, one of them a nephew of Captain James Barry? In his own hand he says so.

GREATEST OF MEN—WASHINGTON

Washington was not a bigot, and no twisting of his birthday can discover him in the garb of one.

The Alexandrians, with disfavor, would hear about the journeying back and forth between the Catholic college and Mt. Vernon. There would be some thoughtless gossip, wincing and grimaces. Washington, the Mason, with many of his dearest and closest friends residing in Alexandria and meeting him there regularly at the lodge, would have to pass through that wonderful old "city" on his way to Georgetown. He would not mind the gossip. His soul was free.

CHAPTER XXX

WASHINGTON'S LOVE OF WASHINGTON

LITTLE voices tell us that Washington pandered to his vanity. The looking-glass gave him celestial consolations. He would have more portraits of himself than any other living man of his time and none but the most distinguished artists would execute them. The proof of this lies in the omnipresence of Washington prints, engravings, crayons, canvases and busts.

Charles Wilson Peale, Robert Edge Pine, Christian Gülager, Edward Savage, John Trumbull, Gilbert Stuart, Jean Antoine Houdon, have been immortalized through Washington's love of his own countenance, head and person. Did not an enthusiastic Frenchman declare that he had the finest legs ever seen on man? Did not another exclaim that his features were so exquisitely proportioned that his face was actually without distinguishing features? Did not Stuart declare that his eye-sockets alone were unlike any he had ever seen in the flesh?

Peale himself informed Thomas J. Bryan that Washington's figure was so superbly proportioned, so majestic, that it had the correct Greek tapering

GREATEST OF MEN—WASHINGTON

from the shoulders to the hips, like the Apollo Belvidere. Bryan was the connecting link between Peale's measurements and the work of the sculptor, H. K. Brown, whose equestrian statue of Washington, after numerous corrections, was finally unveiled July 4, 1856, in Union Square, New York City, where it promises to stand forever.

The same Bryan was the donor of the collection of portraits of Washington now to be seen in the galleries of the New York Historical Society. It was to him that Peale revealed the true color of Washington's eyes. Stuart made them a clear blue gray because he had no ultramarine or other mineral blue that would secure a permanent gray, and he knew that the animal blue he used would eventually become gray. Washington's eyes were light gray and Stewart's misrepresentation was temporary in intention as he believed that the color he used would eventually fade into the true gray.

Of course Washington was conscious of the singular grace and nobility of his person. The pits of smallpox which alone "disfigured" him were neither numerous nor deep. He had a slight scar on the left cheek and a little mole under the right ear seemingly set there to stress the elegance and perfection to which they called attention all the more, as does a black point a woman's beauty.

No one may guess how often Martha reminded

WASHINGTON'S LOVE OF WASHINGTON

him that he was the handsomest being in America. Douglas Fairbanks and Richard Mansfield had bodies suggestive of the symmetry and vitality of Washington's if we allow for the reduced scale upon which they were drawn. But Washington's head and face were Caesar-like in dignity and power, with the august serenity and benignity that Caesar lacked.

Washington at his shaving-glass could see the reflection of what he was. Surely he could not be blind to the image encountered by his eyes. He must have been vain. The pictures and the busts are so many testimonials revealing the laced, embroidered, fringed and tasselled vanity of vanities.

But how came he to sit so often? And what did he think of the extraordinary pictures that grew before him as he sat? His diary tells the whole astounding tale, but nowhere reveals a hint of his satisfaction or dissatisfaction. Even pictures that were obviously not good did not arouse a comment, and he permitted them to go into circulation without protest. One artist returns after two years to make corrections. Washington frankly and simply does not care.

The famous Peale comes to Mt. Vernon, May 18, 1772. Washington is in his fortieth year. The picture that results is the first of which we have an accurate record. But Mr. Peale is not permitted to leave Mt. Vernon until he has painted a miniature of Martha and two more of the children.

It was Washington's custom to go hunting with "Jacky," as he called him, and he wanted "Jacky's" portrait.

April 28, 1785, Mr. Pine, the English artist, arrives at Mt. Vernon, but the very next day Washington, age 53, is in his saddle to Fredericksburg, sixty miles off, visiting his mother. He does not return until May 6. He finds everybody well except little "Jacky." He also finds Mr. Pine, who continues to partake of his hospitality for three weeks. About the pictures, nothing; and we hear no more of Mr. Pine until July 1, 1787, and all we get is this: "Set this morning for Mr. Pine, who wanted to correct his portrait of me." The artist, not Washington, is concerned.

It is fifteen years since we have heard of Mr. Peale, but now in April, 1787, he wishes to make a "Mezzotinto" print.

Who is responsible for the Gülager and Trumbull pictures? Washington, age 57, is in Boston, October 27, 1789. The Committee of the Town insist that he shall sit for his picture to be hung in Faneuil Hall, "that others might be copied from it for the use of their respective families."

Washington's vanity moves him to regret that he cannot delay sufficiently but promises he "will have

WASHINGTON'S LOVE OF WASHINGTON

it (the picture) drawn when returned to New York, if there was a good Painter there—or by Mr. Trumbull when he should arrive, and would send it to them."

Perhaps Boston isn't sufficiently metropolitan to provide an artist worthy of the issue. Perhaps Washington is excusing himself until he can find greater talent. Absurd suspicion. He moves on to Portsmouth, N. H., scarcely to be ranked with Boston in prestige. There November 2, 1789, he sits two hours for Gülager, and leaves Portsmouth "quietly and without any attendance, having earnestly entreated that all parade and ceremony might be avoided."

But what about the Savage portrait? Joseph Willard, president of the University of Cambridge, demands Washington's picture. So, December 21 and 28, 1789, and January 6, 1790, he sits for Mr. Savage. Everybody wants his picture. The vice-president of the United States must have one, so in the following April, Washington patiently sits again for Mr. Savage.

All through February, March and July of 1790 he sits for Mr. Trumbull "to draw my picture in his historical series." He exercises on horse-back "attended by Mr. John Trumbull, who wanted to see me mounted." No man may forget that this artist has been a soldier and has had a stormy career. He

GREATEST OF MEN—WASHINGTON

has actually been imprisoned in the Tower in reprisal for the execution of Major André. Now of course the war is over.

Mr. Trumbull has become fascinated by his subject. He will make a full length portrait (the one now at Yale) to present to Mrs. Washington. This finishes the portrait business, until Washington's 65th year, except for a brief note in January, 1797: "Road to Germantown with Mrs. Washington to see Mr. Stuart's paintings." There is not a word as to when he sat for the Stuart pictures, not a hint whether he liked them or not.

In 1785, at the age of fifty-two, when he is physically at his best, the vain man writes whimsically of his vanity:

"In for a penny, in for a pound, is an old adage. I am so hackneyed to the touches of the painter's pencil, that I am now altogether at their beck; and sit like Patience on a monument while they are delineating the lines of my face. It is a proof, among many others, of what habit and custom can accomplish. At first I was as impatient at the request, and as restive under the operation, as a colt is of the saddle. The next time I submitted very reluctantly, but with less flouncing. Now, no dray-horse moves more readily to his thill than I to the painter's chair."

All this is of the very essence of vanity. True enough, if the romancers are to pronounce the judgment.

WASHINGTON'S LOVE OF WASHINGTON

In the meantime we must not be too sure about his toothless gums, for years afterwards he tells how he stayed at home all day with a toothache, his gum much swollen. False teeth there were, but the gums were not toothless. How could he have munched on walnuts for hours at a time, without teeth to help him? False teeth don't ache. Yes, there were false teeth but how long before the end we do not know.

CHAPTER XXXI

WASHINGTON'S COLDNESS TO HIS MOTHER

WASHINGTON has no love for his mother, yet of all her sons he is the one who looks after her. Fredericksburg, where she lives, is sixty miles from Mt. Vernon. Incessantly, in season and out of season, he makes the trip on horse-back to see her. There are no macadam roads, no broad highways, no smooth, manicured turnpikes. His horses flounder in the dirt and mud, but you will find the record of his systematic visits written in his own hand. He ferries the Occoquan, crosses the Neabsco, Quantico, Choppawamsic, Aquia and Potomac Creeks. It is a rough ride, but you will find him taking it cheerfully throughout the four volumes of his diary. The woman who bore him gave him his frame, his heart, his character. He who knew human nature so well knew two women better —his wife and his mother. To Martha he owed continuity. To his mother he owed beginning.

The management of her plantation is constantly on his mind. Apart from her income in her own right he continually delivers cash to her in his own hand. She is a stern woman, inflexible, imperious,

WASHINGTON'S COLDNESS TO HIS MOTHER

but beautifully simple. Her wants are few. Really she has no wants. Her son knows this. He does not try to surround her with artificialities to which she can never become endeared, yet he is solicitous and eager.

In 1774, while engaged in the heavy business at Philadelphia, he makes sentimental purchases including a riding chair and a cloak for "mother."

Martha and her mother-in-law were not good friends, the little voices tell us, yet in all the years during which Washington attends the House of Burgesses, accompanied by Martha and the children, they take advantage of the trip to Williamsburg and make it the occasion of "visiting mother." To be sure, Williamsburg is much farther than Fredericksburg, but if there is estrangement between Martha and the mother of George, Martha can find excuse for avoiding the longer trip, knowing that it means an uncomfortable experience on the way at Fredericksburg.

The Washingtons are not welcome at Mt. Vernon! Martha, according to the little voices, will have only her own relatives about her. Wholly false! Miserably false! These two women were women indeed. Without fuss they admired, revered and loved each other. Washington's relatives were dear to Martha for her husband's sake. Perhaps she had to bear with some of them, but, if so, the world never knew and they were always in her house. What a light upon the woman's character and upon his!

Washington's diary is crammed with records of the visits to Mt. Vernon of Anne Washington; Augustine Washington, George's half-brother; Bushrod Washington, his nephew; Mrs. Bushrod Washington; Katie Washington, daughter of Warner Washington; Kitty Washington, Charles Washington, Corbin Washington, Mrs. Corbin Washington, Betsy Washington, Ferdinando Washington, George Augustine Washington and his wife; George Corbin and George Steptoe Washington; Henry, Hannah and Jane Washington; John Washington of Stafford; John Augustine Washington and his wife; young John Augustine, the son of Corbin Washington; Lawrence Washington of Belmont, not the half-brother with whom he went to Barbados; Lawrence Washington of Cantako; Lawrence Washington of Fairfax County; Lawrence Washington, the brother of Lund Washington; Lawrence Washington, Jr.; Lawrence Washington, George's nephew; Millie Washington, Needham Washington, Pollie Washington, Richard and Robert and Samuel Washington, and Samuel's wife; nephew Samuel; Sarah, Thomas and Thornton Washington; Townsend, Warner and Mrs. Warner Washington; Whiting Washington; William, the nephew and William the half-brother of

WASHINGTON'S COLDNESS TO HIS MOTHER

George; Colonel William and William Augustine Washington.

He fishes, goes fox-hunting, plays cards, with all these Washingtons at Mt. Vernon. Martha does not sulk and go upstairs. She presides at the dinners. The suggestion of a family feud is a small suggestion and should not be noticed here, nor would it be so noticed were it not for what it reveals of the true Washington, and of Martha!

October 15, 1785, he writes: "After the Candles were lighted George Auge. Washington and Frances Bassett were married by Mr. Grayson." His letter to Frances Bassett's father reveals the antithesis of a Washington feud at the Mt. Vernon mansion. He wants his nephew and his bride to make their home under the same roof with Martha and himself. Let the happy sentiment reveal its charm in Washington's own words:

"My nephew, G. Aug. Washington is just returned . . . apparently much amended in his health but not quite free from the disorder in his breast. I have understood that his addresses to your Daughter were made with your consent; and now I learn that he is desirous, and she is willing to fulfil the engagement they have entered into; and that they are applying to you for permission therefor. It has ever been a maxim with me thru life, neither to promote nor to prevent a matrimonial connexion, unless there should be something

GREATEST OF MEN—WASHINGTON

indispensably requiring an interference . . . ; I have always considered marriage as the most interesting event of one's life—the foundation of happiness or misery. —to be instrumental therefore in bringing two people together who are indifferent to each other, and may soon become objects of hatred—or to prevent a union which is prompted by mutual esteem and affection—is what I never could reconcile to my feelings, and therefore, neither directly nor indirectly have I ever said a syllable to Fanny or George on the subject of their intended connexion; but as their attachment to each other seems to have been early formed, warm and lasting, it bids fair to be happy: if, therefore, you have no objections, I think the sooner it is consummated the better. —I have just now informed them (the former thru Mrs. Washington) that it is my wish they should live here."

This letter obviously written with Martha's full consent and approval, for she was party to it, reveals Washington in a role of human sympathy and wisdom and Martha by his side conspiring with him to make it easy not for her own niece or nephew, but for the nephew of her husband and the object of his affections to dwell together all under the same roof. The letter was written May 23. Within less than five months the marriage ceremony was performed.

Martha was completely surrounded by Wash-

WASHINGTON'S COLDNESS TO HIS MOTHER

ingtons, as Washington himself was completely surrounded by Dandridges and Custises, his wife's relatives. Perhaps such intimacies are dangerous, but neither George nor Martha thought so. Certainly in the record of them can be found no fiber out of which to weave a family feud.

And what shall we say of this insignificant entry in Washington's "Cash Memorandum Book A"? He is about to enter the war. He journeys to Fredericksburg to see his mother. It may or may not be for the last time. He will leave some little gratuity for the old negress who serves the woman who bore him. "By my Mother for the Granny at her Quarter 10s."

Just such little things as these, commonly overlooked by gossipers, tell what manner of man Washington really was. He would bring a smile to the face of old Granny. Perhaps she would be all the kinder to his mother in memory of it. Washington was not a good actor. When bored he could not conceal his impatience. He would try, but awkwardly. There was no self-exhibitionism in him. What he did was wholly spontaneous. The petty episode concerning that trifling gratuity to old Granny is worthy of its place in history for even by the light of a tallow candle a Raphael may be seen. The ten shillings are overflowing with the love of a son, a great son, for a mother, a great

GREATEST OF MEN—WASHINGTON

mother, and they are spilled into the lap of an aging negress.

We may forget all about Plato and his dictum to the effect that man derives his character through his mother. Washington may or may not have been familiar with Plato but he knew and his mother knew and his elder half-brother knew. That halfbrother, because he did know, willed Mt. Vernon not to his mother but to the young George whom he loved as a son and trusted as a father. There is a devastating event! Its significance is overwhelming! The love of the boy Washington for his mother was so deep and so obvious that a mere halfbrother, about to die, could leave all to the youngster and go in peace. The youngster would always look after his mother. It wasn't necessary to be ordinarily prudent in making that will. Such a mother and such a son! And such a half-brother! Testimony coming down the years to reveal the truth to two little men; to neutralize the poison of their fountain pens; to inspire a generation which has all but forgotten filial devotion to a new love— a new concept of life—a new world!

CHAPTER XXXII

A MYTH CANNOT CREATE

WASHINGTON was all luck. Fortune smiled upon him. He scarcely understood that his soul was instinct with destiny. True enough he was a man of affairs managing not only his own and his mother's plantations, but also the estates of his stepchildren inherited from their father. It is a mere coincidence that the estates were handled so ably that young "Jacky" at the age of twenty-one found himself the wealthiest youth in the colony.

Washington was favored by fate. His drainage and lumber operations carried on for five years as a business enterprise in the Dismal Swamp must have been fictions. Perhaps as head of the James River Company and president of the Potomac River Company he was content to dream.

There may be two souls in America at this hour who do not believe that in 1784 Washington prevented the disintegration of the ceaselessly hostile and constantly fighting States which survived the Revolution. There may be two souls in America who doubt that Washington made the Constitutional Convention possible. The same two souls

GREATEST OF MEN—WASHINGTON

may not believe that from the medley of horns and hoofs goring and trampling each other Washington built a government where there was none—a government so stable, so wisely founded, that after eight years of his management it could function without him, growing in a brief hundred years to the mightiest political enterprise the world has ever seen.

The same two souls may disagree with the historical fact that Washington, espousing the cause of Alexander Hamilton against terrific opposition, became the father of America's national banks.

They may not know that Washington visioned the nation evolved by him from chaos and prophesied its greatness. They may not know that he foresaw Henry Ford at Detroit.

Let them go to his diary for October, 1784: "Detroit is a point, thro' which the Trade of the Lakes Huron, and all those above it, must pass, if it centers in any State of the Union."

He is addressing himself to transportation and the significance of transportation to the development of the far west.

"Let us open a good communication with the Settlements west of us—extend the inland Navigation as far as it can be done with convenience—and shew them by this means, how easy it is to bring the products of their Lands to our Markets, and see

A MYTH CANNOT CREATE

how astonishingly our exports will be increased; and these States benefitted in a commercial point of view —wch. alone is an object of such Magnitude as to claim our closest attention—but when considered in the political point of view, it appears of much greater importance.

"No well informed Mind need be told . . . how necessary it is to apply the cement of interest to bind all parts of the United territory together by one indissoluble band—particularly the middle States—with the Country immediately back of them. —For what ties, let me ask, should we have upon those people; and how entirely unconnected shod. we be with them if the Spaniards on their right or great Britain on their left, instead of throwing stumbling blocks in their way as they now do, should invite their trade and seek alliances with them? What, when they get strength, which will be sooner than is generally imagined, may be the consequence of their having formed such connections and alliances requires no uncommon foresight to predict.

"The Western Settlers stand as it were on a pivot —the touch of a feather would almost incline them any way."

So he goes on describing the combination of circumstances that make the present conjuncture more favorable than any other to fix the trade of the Western Countries to our Markets.

He speaks of the private views of some individ-

GREATEST OF MEN—WASHINGTON

uals in sympathy with the court of G. Britain to retain the posts of Oswego, Niagara, Detroit—an infraction of the spirit of the treaty and injurious to the Union, though done under its letter. "The way is plain," he says, "and the expense, comparatively speaking, deserves not a thought, so great would be the prize."

He tells how to avoid complications, how to open wide the door and make smooth the way.

"If we wanted proof of this, look to the avidity with which we are renewing, after a total suspension of Eight years, our correspondence with Great Britain;—so, if we are supine, and suffer without a struggle the Settlers of the Western Country to form commercial connections with the Spaniards, Britons, or with any of the States in the Union, we shall find it a difficult matter to dissolve them."

He actually sees the modern system of transportation "working Boats against stream, by mechanical powers . . . one of those circumstances which have combined to render the present epoche favorable above all others for securing a large portion of the produce of the Western Settlements."

Perhaps it is difficult to associate Washington with a mental picture of mechanical means of transportation; of the phenomenal growth of the United States at a time when the United States had no

A MYTH CANNOT CREATE

government and, despite the success of the Revolution, threatened never to have one, so violent were the forces of jealousy and greed conspiring against a union.

There is no need to repeat what has been said ten thousand times. Washington, the farmer, characterized before his greatness had been established, as "the greatest man" in the colonies by no less an authority than Patrick Henry, worked with his hands, heart and head, with no model before him but the vision in his own soul. What he accomplished is here. A myth can neither foresee nor create. Washington did both.

CHAPTER XXXIII

WASHINGTON'S IRISH PREJUDICE

WASHINGTON was the most eminent Mason of his age, perhaps of any age. Why should a free-thinker join up with the Masonic body? The times were filled with cries of "No Popery!" Religious animosities and racial prejudices were ever spitting fire. The Irish were a proscribed and despised race of foreigners and intruders. They were doubly dangerous because they were singularly Catholic. Give them half a chance and the Pope would soon be in possession of the colonies. Obviously Washington entered the Masonic Order for no purpose save that of defending America against the sinister machinations of the Holy See.

To keep anti-papal fervor at white heat it was customary to burn the effigy of the Pope as often as occasion warranted occasion. Steeped in bigotry, Washington's reactions, because he was so intensely human, had to be human reactions. As all were doing he would do. His interest in the Masonic Order was but a flash of his fear of Rome.

To the astoundment of all engaged in the belittling of Washington the cold facts, rarely warmed

WASHINGTON'S IRISH PREJUDICE

over for human consumption, should forever banish all suspicion of his tolerance. The "Al Smiths" of the seventeenth and eighteenth centuries had no terrors for him.

Long before the war was dreamed of he knew the history of Thomas Dongan, Earl of Limerick, general in the armies of England and France, governor of New York for five years, father of the first representative Assembly and the Charter of Rights and Privileges, which granted popular government, religious toleration, trial by jury, immunity from martial law and freedom from arbitrary arrest.

Washington knew that the same Thomas Dongan, Catholic governor of New York, was the framer of the first City Charters for Albany and New York, and the founder of a Latin School conducted under Catholic auspices by Catholic teachers, and yet had never attempted to seize the government for the Pope.

It made no difference whatsoever to Washington whether an Irishman or the son of an Irishman was Catholic or Protestant. He was interested neither in the shape nor the color of the vessel. The important thing was what it contained. James Moore, grandson of Rory O'More, had been governor of Carolina. When Washington was married Arthur Dobbs, a native of Carrickfergus was governor of North Carolina. Ten years later Matthew Rowan,

GREATEST OF MEN—WASHINGTON

another native of Carrickfergus, was governor of the same State. During the Revolution Thomas Rutledge and Thomas Burke, both of them born in Ireland, were governors of South Carolina. Washington knew that eighteen years before his birth John Hart, born in County Cavan, had become governor of Maryland. He also knew that John McKinley, a native of Ireland, was elected governor of Delaware in 1776. He might have foretold that James Duane, the son of an Irishman, would be the first mayor of the city of New York after the Revolution.

We are not greatly surprised when we find Washington, the Mason, selecting Colonels Hand, Magaw, Haslet and Shea, all born in Ireland, to command the regiments covering the retreat of the American forces after the terrible route at Long Island. Those who would verify the fact may refer to Lieutenant-Colonel James Chambers, Pennsylvania Archives, 5th Ser., Vol. II, p. 612.

As we become accustomed to truth our surprise imperceptibly diminishes in the discovery that preconceived ideas bear so little resemblance to nature. Consequently we scarcely notice George Washington and his Adjutant-General Edward Hand as they affix their signatures to the membership roll of the Society of the Friendly Sons of St. Patrick of Philadelphia, nor do we consider it strange that

WASHINGTON'S IRISH PREJUDICE

Washington, about to enter Boston as Howe prepares to leave, makes "St. Patrick" the countersign.

If Washington feared the Irish or the Pope why did he have men about him like Captain John Brady, the scout; Timothy Murphy, the flaming light of Saratoga; Major Jack Kelly who destroyed the bridge at Stony Brook during the retreat from Trenton, thus preventing the annihilation of the Americans by the British; Lieutenant Jimmy Gibbons, glorified at the storming of Stony Point; Captain Billy O'Neill who stopped the British at the Battle of Brandywine?

Surely not because he had to break them for cowardice or graft; not because their spirit was mercenary; not because they would not march boldly up to a works or stand exposed in a plain. Of the New England troops he wrote from Cambridge, August 20, 1775, to Lund Washington:

"I have already broke one Colonel and five Captains for Cowardice, or for drawing more Pay and Provisions than they had men in their companies; two more Colonels now under arrest to be tried for the same offences; in short they are by no means such Troops, in any respect, as you are led to believe of them from the accounts which are published, but I need not make myself enemies among them by this declaration, although it is consistent with truth."

GREATEST OF MEN—WASHINGTON

General Philip Schuyler complained similarly two years later, August 10, 1777, to Congress against the Connecticut and Massachusetts militia. There were no such complaints against Washington's Irish troops, though many years later the historian Bancroft did make an abortive effort to suppress, distort and misrepresent the truth. Bancroft, not Washington, revelled in prejudice. General Henry Lee who fought in the Revolution, and who, after the war, became governor of Virginia, was without prejudice. In his Memoirs, published nine years after Washington's death, Vol. II, p. 203, he stated simply: "The Line of Pennsylvania might have been, with more propriety, called the Line of Ireland . . . singularly fitted for close and stubborn action, hand to hand in the center of the army."

Americans who have been impressed by the calumnies of Bancroft will quickly efface his unworthy and ungrateful marks by consulting Washington himself.

So important had the Irish become to Washington that March 17, 1781, and March 17, 1782, the feast of St. Patrick, was officially celebrated by the troops. But these Irishmen were Scotch-Irish Orangemen! Who ever heard of Orangemen celebrating the feast of St. Patrick? Who ever heard of Scotch-Irish celebrating March 17?

The diary of Colonel Israel Angell of the Second

WASHINGTON'S IRISH PREJUDICE

Rhode Island Regiment contains this entry: "Good weather; a great parade this day with the Irish, it being St. Patrick's. I spent the day on the Point (West Point) and tarried with the officers."

The journal of Lieutenant William Feltman of the First Regiment of the Pennsylvania Line reveals this entry the following year:

"This morning received an invitation from Lt. Smith to spend St. Patrick's day with him in company with Lt. North, Lt. McCollam, Lt. Reed, Dr. McDowell, Ensigns Van Cort and Cunningham . . . at Kennedy's, fifteen miles from Camp, twelve miles from Charleston, and spent the day and greater part of the night very agreeably."

Washington wrote freely in his bitterness against the make-believe virtues of thousands of his troops. How different the character of his reference December, 1781, to his Irish, when he writes:

"I accept with singular pleasure the Ensign of so worthy a fraternity as that of the Sons of St. Patrick . . . , a society distinguished for the firm adherence of its members to the glorious cause in which we are embarked . . . I shall never cast my eyes upon the badge with which I am honored but with a grateful remembrance . . ."

Was it because his great generals, Wayne, Butler, Hand, Irvine and Moylan, were members of the

GREATEST OF MEN—WASHINGTON

Philadelphia society that January 1, 1782, he attended its banquet and the following March was again to be found at the table of the Friendly Sons, then celebrating St. Patrick's day? This was no new enthusiasm for the Irish, for at the banquet given by the officers of General Sullivan's forces in the Wyoming Valley, September 25, 1779, it was Lafayette himself who proposed the toast: "May the Kingdom of Ireland merit a stripe in the American Standard."

CHAPTER XXXIV

BURNING THE POPE IN FIRE

EVERYBODY knows how the Irish, after five years' fighting, mutinied in the Pennsylvania lines. Washington himself, in his letter to Rochambeau, January 20, 1781, declares the trouble was due to "the absolute want of pay and clothing (and) the great scarcity of provisions." Then he adds this astonishing sentence: "It is somewhat extraordinary that these men, however lost to a sense of duty, had so far retained that of honor, as to reject the most advantageous proposition from the enemy."

Everybody does not know that after the trouble General Wayne wrote Washington: "The disbanded soldiers (The Line of Ireland) were as importunate to be re-enlisted as they had been to be discharged; a reclaimed and formidable Line was the result in the spring."

Who can explain Washington's partiality to the Irish, a despised and submerged race of foreigners, with whose religion nobody in the colonies was in sympathy; whose descendants later, when seeking

GREATEST OF MEN—WASHINGTON

employment, were confronted by signs reading: "No Irish Need Apply"?

When Washington wrote to Rochambeau, August 26, 1780, rejoicing over "the intelligence of the Irish Militia's driving the English out of the forts" he was contributing to what afterwards became "A Hidden Phase of American History," thus making it possible for Michael J. O'Brien to bring to light more than a hundred years later the extraordinary attachment of the great general to his Irishmen.

Perhaps Washington's partiality to the children of Erin was due to their nuisance value. But they had no nuisance value after the war. How, then, are we to explain his entertainment at Mt. Vernon of a young student of Georgetown College, the nephew of Captain James Barry, according to some authorities; the nephew of Commodore John Barry, father of the American Navy, born in Wexford, Ireland, according to others? How truth arises to remove the tarnish from Washington's name! "There were not 300 real Celts in the Revolutionary army" says the famous historian whose love of truth was so infirm that by implication he would hazard another calumny at Washington's expense rather than bury a prejudice. If there were not 300 real Celts in the Revolutionary army Washington padded the Muster Rolls with fictitious names; padded the Continental expense ac-

BURNING THE POPE IN FIRE

count with fictitious pay; put into his pocket the graft thus collected by himself while he was arresting and courtmartialling unfaithful colonels and captains for doing the same thing.

Here, indeed, is a theme for the 1926 biographers and their ilk.

W. C. Ford's alleged life of Washington, designed to strip him of some of his glory, has been blown to bits by Schroeder-Lossing. Edward C. Towne describes the Ford attack as

"Executed on lines deliberately and avowedly intended to bring Washington down from his high historic pedestal; and in sequel to this Mr. Ford's brother undertook a popular volume, designed to reduce Washington from the heroic, almost godlike level, to that of a common historical character."

The 1926 biographers have not been blown to bits and they have reduced Washington to a level so low as to be indescribable. There is only one more notch in the descent. The tabulation of figures about to follow will enable them to reach that notch by bringing out a volume devoted to "George Washington's Falsifications of the Official Payroll of the Revolutionary Army and the Enormous Profits Gained by Him through Padding the Expense Account of the War."

To begin with, his padding was done boldly, ar-

[201]

GREATEST OF MEN—WASHINGTON

rogantly, contemptuously. He relied upon names that would be questioned, the very flavor of which would justify a challenge. In his imperious folly he selected the very worst names for his own purpose—the very worst that history would be called upon to endure.

In the first place the Irish, whose names enabled him to rob the Continental treasury, had a bad beginning in America. Wherever they went they were sure to find that image of the Pope tied to a stake, licked by a blazing fire. They were merely names, mind you—padding on a payroll. Yet Washington became obsessed by the necessity of protecting the pad. That he and Benjamin Franklin sought the aid of the French Catholics has nothing to do with a padded payroll; it is merely historical fact.

Whatever the motive, he would have to quench those anti-Catholic fires—fires that to this day continue to sparkle in flaming crosses lit by 100 per cent Americans in hood and gown. The quenching would express his shrewd recognition of the folly of giving offense to men whose aid was sadly needed by the anti-Popery torch-bearers. True the names were fictitious, but he would have to act toward them as if they were real. Thus, having set the stage for himself with all its paste-board props, he came to the famous "Order of November 5th." And here's the Order:

BURNING THE POPE IN FIRE

"As the commander-in-chief has been apprized of a design formed for the observance of that ridiculous and childish custom of burning the effigy of the Pope, he cannot help expressing his surprise that there should be officers and soldiers in this army so void of common sense, as not to see the impropriety of such a step at this juncture; at a time when we are soliciting and have really obtained the friendship and alliance of the people of Canada, whom we ought to consider as brethren embarked in the same cause, the defense of the general liberty of America.

"At such a juncture and in such circumstances, to be insulting their religion, is so monstrous as not to be suffered or excused; indeed instead of offering the most remote insult, it is our duty to express public thanks to these our brethren, as to them we are so much indebted for every late happy success over the common enemy in Canada."

But whose religion is being insulted? The religion of the padded payroll, of course.

Washington's conscienceless design upon the funds of the Congress involves the fictitious names of 13,193 Irish officers and soldiers divided into groups as follows:

First group—99 Barrys, 127 Bradys, 93 Brennans, 187 Brynes and Byrnes, 221 Burkes, 150 Callahans, 62 Cassidys, 183 Carrolls, 104 Caseys, 69 Cavanaughs, 155 Cains, Canes, Kanes, McKeans and O'Keans, 37 Clancys, 54 Crowleys, 243 Connollys, 327 Connors and O'Connors.

GREATEST OF MEN—WASHINGTON

Second group—205 Dalys and Daileys, 71 Delaneys, 72 Dempseys, 73 Donohues, 155 Donnollys, 38 Dorans, 72 Donovans, 58 Dowlings, 125 Doyles, 42 Driscolls and Driskells, 248 Doughertys, 78 Duffys, 90 Dugans and Duggans, 57 Dwyers and Dwires, 142 Farrells, 184 Fitzgeralds, 67 Fitzpatricks, 36 Fitzsimmonses, 59 Flannigans, 138 Flynns.

Third group—108 Gallaghers, 54 Gormans, 45 Gradys and McGradys, 62 Haggertys, 86 Healys and Haeleys, 44 Hennesys, 115 Hogans, 53 Hurleys, 695 Kellys, 92 Kearneys and Carneys, 64 Keatings, 164 Kenneys and McKennys, 44 Keefes.

Fourth group—61 Laffertys, 94 Learys, 128 Lynches, 81 Maddens, 76 Malones, 89 Mahoneys, 97 Maloneys, 165 Magees and McGees, 97 Magraths, McGraths and McGraws, 44 Morans, 40 Mulhollands, 108 McBrides, 89 Malloys, 74 Mooneys, 494 Murphys.

Fifth group—39 McCaffreys and McCafferys, 88 McCanns, 180 McConnells and Connells, 331 McCarthys, 154 McCormacks, 45 McCloskeys, 47 McDermotts, 34 McDonoughs, 139 McDonalds and McDaniels, 72 McGahys and McGahans, 112 McGinnisses, 69 McGowans, 168 McGuires, 223 McLaughlins, 143 McMahons, 72 McManuses.

Sixth group—231 Mullens, Mullins and McMullens, 90 McNallys, 47 McNamaras, 90 Nolans and Nolands, 36 O'Donnells, 58 O'Haras, 40 Prender-

BURNING THE POPE IN FIRE

gasts, 48 Quigleys, 122 Quinns, 44 Regans, 69 Roches and Roaches, 38 Rourkes, 73 Sheas and Shays, 66 Sheehans, 41 Sheridans, 115 Sweeneys and McSweeneys, 201 Walshes and Welches.

Here we have the ghosts of 13,193 witnesses testifying from the Muster Rolls of the Revolutionary Army to the rascality and greed of the man who did the padding and pocketed the spoils. If perchance the payroll was not padded why, then, have we never had in America a Society known as the American Sons and Daughters of the Irish Continentals? Certain it is that Washington's padded payroll narrowly escaped detection shortly after his death. *The Aurora* of February 27, 1800, contains this: "Three-fifths of the men enlisted were Irish immigrants." The same *Aurora* is frequently quoted by Claude G. Bowers in his *Jefferson and Hamilton* in which the Irish are described p. 484 as "the most God-provoking Democrats this side of hell."

CHAPTER XXXV

WASHINGTON THE UN-AMERICAN

IT is not enough to assail Washington's greatness in Greenwich village whispers such as "He made Martha sleep up in the attic," or "I was so afraid you'd repeat one of the other little stories you no doubt heard about him—I mean the spicy ones, which I don't think we ought to mention, because after all, you know, Washington, though intensely human, was the father of his country."

That Martha never slept up in the attic until after Washington's death, and that the reason she took the room under the roof was because it contained the only window of the house sufficiently elevated to enable her to look down upon the vault wherein, with Masonic rites, they buried him, is a truth entirely too old-fashioned and unsophisticated to offset the ridiculous story.

For the other pornographic rumors it can be said that no living man's great-great-grandfather whispered them to his great-grandfather, who in turn whispered to his grandfather, so that in due time his father heard the tale and was able thus to pass

WASHINGTON THE UN-AMERICAN

it on, that now the son may continue the traditional narrative and keep it moving.

The spicy stories are all of recent origin, but because the modern stage, the deformed tabloid newspaper and the scandal courts never cease to belch their salacious vapors, the smart ones of the hour are prone to accept without challenge the "evidence" of a great man's weakness as flattering proof that they themselves resemble the great man at least in this. That thus all resemblance ends does not occur to them. They are Americans.

Washington was not an American. This is a species of attack originating on clean ground. Even Jefferson's differences with Washington were clean. Washington had seemed to make him fumble and had hurt his pride by appearing to repose greater confidence in Jefferson's enemy, Hamilton. The reactions were bitter but without venom.

An intellect as "limited in depth and vision" as the intellect of Washington could not be expected to rise to Jeffersonian heights and so there were whispers, not about Washington's morals, but rather about the inferiority of his mental powers and the thickening of his arteries due to advancing years.

Henry Cabot Lodge explained Pickering's characterization of Washington as "commonplace, not original in his thought, and vastly inferior to Hamilton" on the ground that Washington was not vio-

GREATEST OF MEN—WASHINGTON

lent and could not make up his mind before he knew the facts.

The isolated instances of antagonism and criticism among Washington's contemporaries have all been traced to the thwarted ambitions of the envious and the political animosities of dwarfish souls.

Happily I possess an old book written by David Ramsay, M. D., member of Congress from 1782 to 1786. Strangely enough this old book was published in London, 1807, and thus was as close to Washington as we of 1927 are close to Theodore Roosevelt or Woodrow Wilson. Ramsay was not a Virginian but his South Carolina origin did not remove him from the inner circle who knew Washington, worked with him, lived with him and loved him.

Ramsay's testimony would stand in any court of justice from which the hearsay libels would receive swift dispatch. Listen to Ramsay:

"The person of George Washington was uncommonly tall. Mountain air, abundant exercise in the open country, the wholesome toils of the chase, and the delightful scenes of rural life expanded his limbs to an unusual but graceful and well-proportioned size.

"His exterior suggested to every beholder the idea of strength united with manly gracefulness. His form was noble and his port majestic. No man could approach him but with respect. His frame was robust, his constitution vigorous, and he was capable of enduring great fatigue.

"His passions were naturally strong; with them was his first contest, and over them his first victory. Before he undertook to command others, he had thoroughly learned to command himself. The powers of his mind were more solid than brilliant. Judgment was his forte.

"His faculties resembled those of Aristotle, Bacon, Locke and Newton, but were very unlike those of Voltaire. Truth and utility were his objects. With this view he thought much, and closely examined, in all its relations, every subject on which he was to decide. Neither passion, party spirit, pride, prejudice, ambition, nor interest influenced his deliberation. In making up his mind on great occasions, and many occurred which seemed to involve the fate of the nation, he sought information from all quarters, revolved the subject by night and by day, and examined it in every point of view imaginable.

"Perhaps no man ever lived, who was so often called upon to form a judgment in cases of real difficulty, and who so often formed a right one. Of a thousand propositions he knew how to distinguish the best, and to select among a thousand the individual one most fitted for his purpose. His perseverance overcame every obstacle; his moderation conciliated all opposition; his genius supplied every resource. He knew how to conquer by delay and deserved true praise by despising unmerited cen-

GREATEST OF MEN—WASHINGTON

sure. The whole range of history does not present a character on which we can dwell with such entire unmixed admiration.

"The integrity of Washington was incorruptible. His real and avowed motives were the same; his ends were always upright and his means pure. He was a statesman without guile; and his professions, both to his fellow-citizens and to foreign nations, were uniformly sincere. No circumstances ever induced him to use duplicity.

"By an extraordinary strength of intellect he overstepped the tedious form of the school, and, by the force of a correct taste and sound judgment, seized on the great ends of learning, without the assistance of those means which have been found necessary to prepare less active minds for public business.

"The powers of his mind were in some respects peculiar. He was a great, practical, self-taught genius, with a head to devise and a hand to execute projects of the first magnitude and greatest utility.

"There are few men of any kind, and still fewer of those the world calls great, who have not some of their virtues eclipsed by corresponding vices; but this was not the case with General Washington. He had religion without austerity, dignity without pride, modesty without diffidence, courage without rashness, politeness without affectation, affability without familiarity.

"His private character, as well as his public one, will bear the strictest scrutiny. The friend of morality and religion, he steadily attended on public

WASHINGTON THE UN-AMERICAN

worship; encouraged and strengthened the hands of the clergy; and in all his public acts made the most respectful mention of Providence. In a word he carried from private life into his public administration the spirit of piety and a dependence upon the Supreme Governor of the universe.

"The honors and applause he received from his grateful countrymen would have made almost any other man giddy, but on him they had no mischievous effect.

"The patriotism of Washington was of the most ardent kind, and without alloy. Very different from those clamorous spirits, who, with love of country in their mouths and hell in their hearts, lay schemes for aggrandizing themselves at every hazard, he was one of those who loved their country in sincerity, and who hold themselves bound to consecrate all their talents to its service. Liberty and law, the rights of man and the control of government were equally dear to him and, in his opinion, equally necessary to political happiness. He thought that real liberty could only be maintained by observing the authorities of the laws and giving tone and energy to government.

"He conceived the difference as immense between a balanced republic and a tumultuous democracy, or a faction calling themselves the people. He saw a still greater disparity between a patriot and a demagogue. The deliberate sentiments of the people he highly respected; but their sudden ebullitions made no impression on his well-balanced mind. Trusting for support to the sober second thoughts of the nation, he had the magnanimity to pursue its real interests, in opposition to prevailing prejudices.

"Having accomplished every object for which he re-entered public life, Washington gave for the second time the rare example of voluntarily descending from the first station in the universe, the head of a free people placed there by their unanimous suffrage. To the pride of reigning his soul was superior; to its labors he submitted only for his country.

"For more than forty years of happy wedded love, his high example strengthened the tone of public manners. In the bosom of his family, he had more real enjoyment than in the pride of military command or in the pomp of sovereign power. His character was a constellation of all the talents and virtues which dignify or adorn human nature."

Now they add to their whispers the indictment that he was not an American. We shall see.

CHAPTER XXXVI

OTHER UN-AMERICAN AMERICANS

LOWELL'S Commemoration Ode describes Abraham Lincoln as "the first American." Clarence King in a prefatory note pronounces Lincoln "the first American to reach the lonely height of immortal fame. Before Lincoln there were but two pre-eminent names—Columbus, the discoverer and Washington, the founder; the one an Italian seer, the other an English country gentleman."

Patrick Henry was not an American. Samuel Adams was not an American. Thomas Jefferson was not an American. Charles Carroll of Carrollton was not an American. Benjamin Franklin was not an American. George Washington was an English country gentleman.

True enough there were only four generations of Americans behind Washington, whereas Lincoln could boast of six. Thus comes into the world a new standard of measurement whereby the Americanism of an American may be judged.

Lodge disposes of this fantastic exhibition of snobbery in a single sentence:

GREATEST OF MEN—WASHINGTON

"There are people today whose families have been here for 250 years, and who are as utterly un-American as it is possible to be, while there are others whose fathers were immigrants, who are as intensely American as any one can desire or imagine."

If we admit that Jefferson was an American Democrat we are compelled to admit that Washington was an American Republican. Jefferson gloried in the French Revolution. Through Lafayette, Rochambeau and thousands of gallant Frenchmen who aided Washington, he learned to love France, but when the French Revolution with its anarchy, murder and gutters filled with clotted blood bore down upon mankind Washington shrank from French fancies, French license and French violence. He had been too close to British license and British violence to lose his balance. He knew that liberty lay in neither. So the more Jefferson preached the French ideal the more Washington differed with him, for he saw in blood the perils to his country that modern Americans have seen in Russia, Germany and Mexico.

If Washington, the product of a fourth American generation, the father of the American nation, was not an American but merely an old-fashioned English country gentleman, we are confronted by a dilemma such as no man was ever called upon to solve. Was John Wilkes Booth, the assassin of

OTHER UN-AMERICAN AMERICANS

Abraham Lincoln, an American? Born in America, he was but one generation out of England. Surely the English will not claim him. How, then, can they claim Washington, who was born four generations out of England?

Benedict Arnold is described by the Encyclopedia Britannica as an American soldier born in Norwich, Conn. True enough his ancestors came to America long before the arrival of Washington, but also, true enough, five of his sons and one of his grandsons became soldiers in the British army. One of these sons, James Robertson Arnold, many years after the American Revolution, was created an English knight. The riddle thickens, for we have here the family of an American traitor throwing off its Americanism and reverting to British life and honor.

Woodrow Wilson can scarcely be described as an American. Both his grandfathers were "foreigners," one of them hailing from County Down, in Ireland, the other a Scotchman.

There was something altogether un-American about the first American Congress of 1774, for among its members were Pierse Long, Matthew Thornton and Thomas Fitzsimmons, natives of Limerick; John Sullivan, whose father was born in Ireland; James Duane, son of Anthony Duane of Galway; Edward Hand, a native of King's County;

GREATEST OF MEN—WASHINGTON

William Irvine, fresh from Fermenagh; Charles and Daniel Carroll from Tipperary; Edward Carrington from Mayo; Thomas Burke of Galway; John Armstrong of Donegal; James McHenry of Antrim; Pierse Butler of Kilkenny; Cornelius Harnett of Dublin; Thomas Lynch, John and Edward Rutledge, all natives of Ireland; Kean, Read, Heney and Kearney, sons of Irishmen.

The un-Americanism of the signers of the Declaration of Independence must ever remain one of the wonders of un-Americanism, for among these signers were Smith, Taylor, Rutledge and Thornton, born in Ireland; Carroll, McKean, Read and Lynch, descendants of Irish immigrants.

Altogether un-American was the father of the American Navy, Commodore John Barry of Wexford.

Sad indeed is the spectacle of the un-American commander-in-chief, George Washington, surrounded by his Irish-born generals, James Hogan, John Greaton, Richard Butler, Richard Montgomery, William Irvine, Edward Hand, William Thompson, William Maxwell, and Andrew Lewis. Among his un-American generals, who were sons of Irish immigrants, were James Moore, James Clinton, George Clinton, Joseph Read, and John Sullivan. His Irish-born colonels were Robert Magaw, John Kelley, John Dooly, John Patton, Walter

OTHER UN-AMERICAN AMERICANS

Stewart, John Shee, John Haslet, Thomas Proctor, John Fitzgerald, Hercules Mooney, Pierse Long and Stephen Moylan.

Having failed everywhere in their un-American assaults on the un-American Washington, there does indeed remain this un-American complication to be properly bestowed. If Washington was not an American it follows that we should manifest more patience and sympathy with the 100 per cent modern Americans who depart so far from his standard.

So, too, should we exhibit in charity a greater toleration of their seemingly strange vagaries, because, after all, it may be true that Washington's Americanism was tainted, and their's pure.

From this confusion may arise a new norm of judgment to enable good and sane men to extend generously the approval and acclamation of ilks, sects, groups and clans from which they have hitherto withheld their praise. Washington could break with an English king; shrink from a French lunacy; cling to a German officer; embrace a Polish patriot; protect an Irish sentiment. The accident of nationality meant nothing to him. He could see only the *man!* Perhaps this was un-American. If so, the characterization stands.

CHAPTER XXXVII

WASHINGTON AND THE TERROR

VERY well, then. We shall make Washington American if we must. But by no dint of effort can we make him a democratic American. The 1926 biographer assures us that "his lack of democracy caused him his final conflicts and defeats and most of his final deluges of abuse in his final years."

Washington did indeed bring fuel to the fires of partisanship and political distemper through his denunciation of the "Democratic Societies" and their fantastic worship of French madness. This act constituted "the greatest mistake of his career." Note the juxtaposition of "conflicts and defeats." Note the sickly complexion of conflicts. Good is always in conflict with evil, wherefore, by way of conflict, good is evil. Let us examine the picture.

Americans describing themselves as patriots and lovers of liberty are dancing La Carmagnole in the streets; singing the Marsellaise; spitting in the faces of men believed to be out of sympathy with the mob. Rioting in the theatres of Philadelphia, these liberty-lovers, intoxicated by the French orgy, discover a well-dressed citizen in the pit. The well-

WASHINGTON AND THE TERROR

dressed citizen is an "aristocrat" of course. The liberty-lovers call upon him to arise and bow to the gallery. He will not. Fruit, vegetables and other missiles are pelted at him. Beer bottles are emptied over his head. His lady companion is spattered. Bedlam breaks. The very orchestra is driven into the street. And this is Philadelphia.

France has anathematized all authority. The French altars are to be overthrown; the Christian era abolished; bishops and priests, publicly, will deny all belief in God. Liberty, assuming the hideous shape of unrestrained license, is adored. Reason is wedded to the harlot, and from the union a tutelary deity of "patriotism" is born. Already in December, 1792, Dupont has harangued the convention. "Why," he demands, "with thrones tottering, scepters breaking, kings expiring, are the altars of the gods allowed to stand?" Robespierre, natural offspring of the Terror, high-priest of the New Liberty, anointed custodian of the New Reason, solemnly declares that he alone knows right; that all who differ with him are enemies of the republic and must die.

What's it all about? Washington observes the symptoms with increasing uneasiness. Jefferson has just returned from Paris. John Jay, chief justice, would like a report on the rioting. Jefferson's judgment is warped. He writes John Jay that the riot-

GREATEST OF MEN—WASHINGTON

ing has no "professed connection with the great national reformation going on." Jefferson is quite certain. Any man who doubts the certainty must be suffering from waning mental powers. The condoned deviltries, destined shortly to scourge the world, are merely the work of the "abandoned banditti of Paris." No, sir, these disorders are wholly unrelated to the wise, sane, eager and benevolent reformation now going on. Jefferson, the critic, is blind indeed. Washington is not so blind.

An unhealthy spirit has taken possession of the "Democratic Societies." How long will the hot rash last? How far will it spread? Jefferson glories in the symptoms of "reform." Washington's temperature is normal.

Genêt, Minister of the French Republic, has arrived in America. Getting off his ship at Charleston he is received by the populace with delerious enthusiasm. On he moves to Philadelphia. "Woe to the American," he cries, "who is hostile to revolutionary France."

Oddly enough he is an aristocrat, a very dandy of Versailles, a favorite of Marie Antoinette. Wherever he goes bells are wrung, guns are fired, orators receive him, the people shout and fling their liberty caps into the air and wave French flags. So he arrives in Philadelphia. The streets are congested with the surging mob whose thunderous

WASHINGTON AND THE TERROR

acclamation will not be checked. Drunk with madness this son of the Terror announces that he will make Washington do his bidding. He will go over Washington's head to the people. The people shout all the more.

The Terror has not yet begun to count its heads, but Washington sees, in the violence of American sympathy for the anarchy now wallowing in its own mire, an obsession whose hysteria has nothing in common with liberty or democracy. The very passion of these demonstrations is a libel upon democracy, a senseless mutilation of the spirit in which his own lofty dream of liberty was conceived, a nightmare of irreligion and unreason.

He knows the depths of Jefferson's sympathy with the French cause. He knows that Jefferson, even though disgusted with Genêt, has been feeding, without malice, the outbursts of frenzied friendship for France. He knows that neither he nor Jefferson can foresee the extent nor control the force of the rising tide. He can despise in patience the first wild debauch of red enthusiasm for regicide and anarchy, but he can also count on the second sober thought of the people, provided only that the second sober thought is not strangled at birth by an Unharnessed Fury. He will deliberately offend the fiery spirits responsible for the hectic and inflammatory state of public sentiment. He will denounce the "Democratic Societies."

America clamors for another war with England, clamors for any enormity that will help France; demands that the French flame shall spread; demands conflagration. Strange spectacle! This same America had not been so valiant, so ardent, so patriotic through those dreadful eight years and eight months when Washington in vain was calling for help, stores, powder, men. Yes, Washington knows the frenzy will subside; but he also knows that during the abatement of it incalculable evil will be done. Yes, he will denounce the "Democratic Societies."

England is making it hard. American ships are being outraged. American seamen are being impressed. American cargoes are being confiscated. Turbulence and division of spirit have reached such a height that the most fashionable people of Philadelphia gather at Richardet's Tavern to celebrate the birthday not of George Washington, but of George III. Five British toasts are drunk. Washington is toasted once. "Neutrality" is toasted twice. The old Tories have become articulate. They are no longer afraid to quaff their public bumpers to George III. Respecting Washington they yield him a solitary glass but will somehow restore America to the Crown.

WASHINGTON AND THE TERROR

But back to Washington's denunciation of the "Democraic Societies." By this denunciation he establishes for the hundredth time the pure integrity of his democracy. He who was not afraid to face the wrath of a British king or to lead a rabble army for more than eight years against the trained veterans of the Crown, with only faith in democracy to sustain him, is not now afraid to face the firebrands who call themselves the "Democratic Societies."

Yet a 1926 biographer would have it that "his lack of democracy caused him his final conflicts and defeats and most of his final deluges of abuse in his final years." As there are no premises save those falsely implied, upon which to erect a conclusion so transparently strained, there must be initiated at once a search for the "defeats" gratuitously set forth.

Neutrality *was* maintained. The people *did* return to their senses. The fanatical Genêt became a laughing stock and showed his true mettle by going into hiding. He did not dare return to France to face the monster he professed to love, and in whose worship he had come to America. There *was no war* with England. America did not damn its soul by participating in the Terror. This was "defeat" indeed!

In justice to the immortal Jefferson it must be

GREATEST OF MEN—WASHINGTON

declared that with his own eyes he had seen the hideous state of society in France from which the Terror sprang. From Paris he had written joyously that "the French nation has been awakened by our Revolution." To whom was this joyous letter written? To Washington himself. Jefferson knew Washington would rejoice.

Of 20,000,000 people supposed to be in France, Jefferson asserted: "Nineteen million are more wretched, more accursed in every circumstance of human existence than the most conspicuously wretched individual in the whole United States." He can never be censored by honest men for his sympathy with what appeared to be a dawning reform. Yet there must ever be surprise in his failure to interpret the crazed egoism of Genêt and his crazier conduct in America as a symptom of the morbidity of the Terror so soon to show its bloody spirit to the world.

Apparently not to the very last had Jefferson ever truly succeeded in feeling the pulse of the sansculotte. Never did he look deeply enough into the heart of Dr. Guillotin. When sworn in as president of the United States he took the oath of office wearing the long pantaloons—an innovation of the Terror designed by an idolater of Robespierre and Marat.

Nevertheless Jefferson, who lived as a true aris-

WASHINGTON AND THE TERROR

tocrat, was in all his sympathies a true democrat, and in his soul he loved the first and truest of all democrats, the Washington of his censure. Had it not been for Jefferson's love of Washington we would not now possess Houdon's statue, for it was Jefferson who arranged with Houdon in Paris to come to America—to Mt. Vernon—that the great and good man might forever survive in marble.

Looking back over the years, himself ever an object of violent criticism, he could recall a picture of the serene and stately Washington looking down upon a howling mob damning his appointment of "a driveler and a fool," John Jay, chief justice of the United States. Did the mob not scribble on the walls: "Damn John Jay! Damn everyone who won't damn John Jay! Damn everyone who won't put lights in his windows and sit up all night damning John Jay!"? Did not Jefferson damn Hamilton? Did not Hamilton damn Jefferson? Did not the whole country damn everybody and everything? Do not the damners survive in their offspring? Of course Washington cannot escape. Criticism must be scribbled on the walls. Scandal must be whispered in the halls. Not even he who gives his all to his countrymen is immune. *Who gives his all!*

Washington, aristocrat at heart, gave his all to democracy. The critics find him holding nothing in his hand. Listen to the blazing lines of Jonathan Miller:

"For all you hold in your cold dead hand
Is what you have given away."

Once more to the "Democratic Societies" and "the most dreadful mistake of Washington's career" in denouncing them. Despite the massacres in Paris and the Genêt lunacies in America the politicians would cling to France because "if France is annihilated, as seems to be the desire of the combined powers, sad indeed will the consequences be for America." The politicians were thinking of *themselves* and dared not examine too closely what the thought might involve. Washington, on the other hand, was thinking of America, of right and honor, and had prepared himself to take a stand against an imminent, self-destroying folly. He himself might be destroyed, but out of such destruction the people would come to their senses and America would endure. Of such was the democracy of Washington.

CHAPTER XXXVIII

WASHINGTON THE INFIDEL

AS early as 1837 there arose discussions tending to throw doubts over the religious belief of Washington. For nearly forty years following his death, when hundreds of eye-witnesses to his manner of life were still alive to refute and confound the "newly-discovered evidence" no man could be found bold enough to whisper what he knew to be false. With an interval of two generations to protect the custodians of dogmatic irreligion there was little to fear from the dead and gone contemporaries of the Mt. Vernon farmer. Now that these old insinuations have become progressively vehement and as casual conversation with intelligent moderns reveals the astonishing extent to which a movement of whispers may impress an age that boasts of its intellectual freedom, we must scrutinize the issue in the light of established truth.

There shall be no conjecture here, as there should be none. Washington's religion was between himself and God, and the value of internal evidence, circumstantial evidence and external appearances must be determined in strict accord with the world's

GREATEST OF MEN—WASHINGTON

acceptance of the man of honor or its rejection of the discredited hypocrite.

Washington's pew was in Fairfax parish, at Alexandria, ten miles from his home. He had another pew in Truro parish, at Pohick, seven miles. As early as 1765 he was a vestryman of both parishes, also a member of the Virginia House of Burgesses. May 24, 1774, the House, unusually grave under the threat of impending disaster, passed this order:

"The first day of June should be set apart as a day of fasting, humiliation, and prayer, devoutly to implore the divine interposition for averting the heavy calamity which threatens destruction to civil rights and the evils of civil war."

Was this order designed to impress the superstitious and gullible; to arouse in them sentiments of approval and support so that a group of rash adventurers might be looked upon by them as a group of honest, patriotic and God-fearing men?

Washington had no auto. The road to church was a dirt road, a rutted road, frequently a mud road. Church-going was a matter of seven miles to one, ten to the other, on horse-back. Washington could go to church to be seen of men. But men could not see him *fasting*. Fasting was between himself and God.

Who will ever know what Washington did that

day, June 1, 1774? Did he conform to the externals of the order which he assisted in passing? Did he respect its spirit? The entire world of his day are in their graves, but Washington's diary lives. Let us turn to June 1, 1774. It contains a single entry: "Went to church and *fasted all day.*"

The significance of this one entry is not a whispering significance. It slept in darkness for more than a hundred years before men could dream of interpreting it. Now it steps forth to meet the whisper that no man may interpret.

Then there is the Orderly Book, which, under date of August 3, 1776, contains this:

"That the troops may have an opportunity of attending public worship . . . the General in future excuses them from fatigue duty on Sunday. The General is sorry that the foolish and wicked practise of profane cursing and swearing is growing into fashion. He hopes officers and men will reflect that we can have little hope of the blessings of Heaven on our arms if we insult it by our impiety and folly; added to this it is a vice so mean and low, without any temptation, that every man of sense and character detests and despises it."

In his instructions to the Brigadier-Generals, May 26, 1777, he orders:

"Let vice and immorality of every kind be discouraged. See that the men regularly attend di-

GREATEST OF MEN—WASHINGTON

vine worship. Gaming of every kind is expressly forbidden, as being the foundation of evil, and the cause of many a brave and gallant officer's ruin."

These are high and mighty words, Puritan words. But Washington was neither high nor mighty. He was not a Puritan. He gamed himself, but not at war. Unhappily he knew the consequences of gaming to the poor wretches who to meet their losses risked the cause to which they were sworn by plundering and grafting. The order was not puritanical; it was sane. But what had cursing, swearing, vice and immorality to do with it?

Above all things Washington was consistent. Let us go back to his habits twenty years earlier. He is addressing himself to the inordinate vices, the drunkenness and profanity, which have been charged against the Virginia regiment. Again December, 1756, he is repeating the matter of May 18, 1756, and inscribes his letter:

"To the Speaker of the House of Burgesses."

These are his words:

"My incessant endeavors have been directed to discountenance gaming, drinking, swearing and other vices, with which all camps too much abound; while, on the other, I have used every expedient to inspire a laudable emulation in the officers, and an unerring exercise of Duty in the Soldiers. If the country think they have cause to condemn my con-

WASHINGTON THE INFIDEL

duct . . . it will give me the greatest pleasure to resign a command which I solemnly declare I accepted against my will."

Washington is acting simply and consistently. Even at this early date he is running true to the form displayed twenty years later—forty years later. Did he never drink? Of course he drank, but not intemperately. Like St. Paul he advocated by his own conduct the use, never the abuse, of all things licit.

But did he never utter an oath himself? There seems to be evidence that he did. But only when provocation was stupendous. One wretch felt the withering sting of Washington's rage against his deviltry and stupidity, but the oath uttered, though we have only a vague guess as to its form, gave immediate rise to a profound and contrite sense of its unworthiness and futility.

Had he been a prodigious swearer himself he could not have submitted his person to uproarious ridicule in 1756 or in 1776 by making a hypocritical pretense of curbing the indulgence of others. Accuse him as we may, he was not an unmitigated ass, and we are therefore compelled to conclude, unless we put him down as a transparent fool, that his order against ribald blasphemies and licentiousness was entirely natural and to be expected. To discourage

GREATEST OF MEN—WASHINGTON

looseness of conduct leading to the decay of discipline when discipline meant the very life of liberty he ordered twenty-five lashes without a courtmartial for the profane and reprobate. This was done not that lashes might be applied, but that they might not be necessary. It did not reveal cruelty. Venereal disease is far more cruel than the prophylactic inhibitions employed to prevent it.

In the great World War the American army in France actually put to death a number of American soldiers because "they were reprobate." There was no other reason. When Washington did "cuss" it must have been a spectacular and edifying event out of which the human at last succeeded in lifting up its head.

The Orderly Book of April 18, 1783, orders: "Thanks to Almighty God for all His mercies, particularly for His overruling the wrath of man to His own glory, and causing the rage of war to cease among the nations."

Five years earlier, August 20, 1778, he had written:

"The hand of Providence has been so conspicuous in all this, that he must be worse than an infidel, that lacks faith, and more than wicked, that has not gratitude enough to acknowledge his obligations."

Fourteen years following this he wrote to General Armstrong, March 11, 1792:

WASHINGTON THE INFIDEL

"There never was a people, who had more reason to acknowledge a divine interposition in their affairs, than those of the United States; and I should be pained to believe that they have forgotten that agency, which was so often manifested during our revolution, or that they failed to consider the omnipotence of that God who is alone able to protect them."

Flushed with triumph he had but one thought, when upon the disbanding of the army, June 8, 1783, he wrote to the governors of all the States:

"I now make my earnest prayer that God would have you and the State over which you preside in His holy protection; that He would incline the hearts of the citizens to entertain a brotherly affection and love for one another; to love mercy and to demean ourselves with that charity, humility and pacific temper of mind which were the characteristics of the Divine Author of our blessed religion, and without an humble imitation of whose example in these things we can never hope to be a happy nation."

Here Washington seems to be writing his heart out in an appeal to the twentieth century. What greater inspiration can our modern pulpits find than in the life of this true and ever humble follower of Christ?

Listen to him, August 19, 1789, as he writes this:

GREATEST OF MEN—WASHINGTON

"It affords edifying prospects indeed to see Christians of every denomination dwell together in more charity, and conduct themselves in respect to each other with a more Christian-like spirit than ever they have done in any former age or in any other nation."

Perhaps this was extravagance, but it was honest extravagance, and in it, though he makes no mention of himself, one can see, as Ramsey saw, the influence of his noble life upon his time.

To his dear Lafayette, August 15, 1787, he wrote:

"Being no bigot myself, I am disposed to indulge the professors of Christianity in the church with that road to heaven which to them shall seem the most direct, plainest, easiest and least liable to exception."

He was not a Jew-baiter or a despiser of other sects than his own. Yearning for the true happiness of men he was ever ready to die for them, escaping martyrdom only because, as it very clearly appears, God wanted him to live for a purpose!

There is much more of this. Those who want it may read the famous letter written by Washington's adopted daughter, who lived twenty years under his roof. She tells how he received what he believed to be the Sacrament, and how he knelt at the bedside of her aunt, praying fervently for her recovery.

CHAPTER XXXIX

THE MISCHIEF OF HIS YOUTH

THE mischief of Washington's youth has been lost in mist. Mischief there must have been, but by the time he began making records of his life at the age of sixteen he had already outgrown the vestments of boyhood. Unrestrained exuberance had vanished. Mature before his time he had already come to love serious adventure and to find frivolous entertainment distasteful. Detesting travel for travel's sake, he journeyed eagerly to Barbados, the first and last of his excursions into other lands. His half-brother, dying of tuberculosis, needed the young lad and the young lad went.

With saddle, knapsack, rifle and one companion, Captain Gist, he entered the wilderness, building his own raft, swimming his horse, attaining his goal, measuring out mercy to the savage who shoots at him. Was this to have been expected? In the light of later developments, yes; for as a youngster he had already marvelled over the habits of life of other human creatures, brooding over their problems and what seemed to him the solution of their difficulties.

GREATEST OF MEN—WASHINGTON

The odd accident of this boy's character, incompatible with the immature of the human species, was his dignity. Responding to the noble, he wrote out the crudely translated speech of a savage, making its tones resemble those of an organ. This disposition of his soul to vibrate in harmony with lofty and noble themes expressed itself in elegance easily mistaken by envious and little minds for foppery.

Always in the saddle, he rode as perhaps no other man had "rid," twenty-six days at a stretch, fifty miles a day, without fatigue. He fished, hunted game, played cards, drank wine and fought—but always for a cause.

For taking up arms against the French and Indians he and his companions were promised a reward by the British government. Failing for fifteen years to receive what was his, he never relented his claims until justice had been done. So scrupulous was his division of the belated bounty that neither complaint nor rumor of complaint on the part of those who shared it with him was ever heard by mortal ear.

His attitude toward marriage was grave to the point of reverence. Regarding the bond as indissoluble he refused to influence in the slightest the judgment of any two beings contemplating a "connexion" that meant for them the highest happiness or the lowest misery.

THE MISCHIEF OF HIS YOUTH

Love of children was the outstanding glory of his heart. Martha, who had already borne four babes, two perishing at birth, one sickly unto death, the other far from robust, could bear no more. One of her letters reveals that in a few months she looked forward to giving George an heir. She hoped the babe would be a girl. What happened will never be known. How serious can be guessed, for George himself in another letter discloses that he has given up all hope of offspring. So he was found adopting children and looking after the education of a score.

Illuminating were his rides with little "Jacky" into the woods.

His solicitude for Martha's peace of mind and heart amounted to a passion. The record of this devotion is scattered over his career from the day of his marriage at twenty-six to the night preceding his death at sixty-seven. Knowing he was dying, he would not allow her to get up to alarm the household, lest she might take cold. So exacting was his fidelity to all trusts that out of it can be read his whole moral code. Abominating deceit in every issue of human relations, his sense of honor, reaching to heights rarely attained by man, was incapable of dallying with any temptation bearing upon the integrity of his affections.

There were no secret contests between him and

GREATEST OF MEN—WASHINGTON

the envious. He never flattered, never played with the vanity of lesser men, never whispered. Plotted against, he did not plot. Blandishments and promises were beyond his horizon. Yet, knowing the meaning of rewards, he bestowed them with affection.

All the threads he spun went straight to the cloth. They never spun themselves in defiance of his plans. He could not be entangled, nor could he entangle others. The word "Execrable!" was unknown to him. To whatsoever difficulty arising in his way, he was at once reconciled. There were no painful transitions, no futile lamentations, no squandered luxuries of self-pity. Fortitude, justice, patience and temperance hovered over his tent. He could have been libertine and king, but to himself he would be farmer, to the whole he would be servant, to the unseen he would be conqueror. The sting of the flesh could irritate and inflame. He would quench its fires. Ice and marble were at hand. He would use them against the animal. He would muzzle the beast and put it down.

Of course men would misjudge him, but misjudgment was an evil that would leave him unmoved. The spurious letters of Voss and Vache, published and "republished with greater avidity & perseverance than ever" could not excite him to answer misjudgment—except in charity: "I will

THE MISCHIEF OF HIS YOUTH

never palliate my own faults by exposing those of another."

Ever gracious to the spontaneous and unsophisticated, he was never ungracious to the stilted and pretentious. He could always retire. Unable to laugh at a ribald tale, he could write a hundred words of merriment at the surprising performance of an army cook who discovers at last that "apples will really make a pye."

Inured to suffering and the vicissitudes of violence, he could curse neither the traitor nor the aching tooth; but he could curse an officer who seemingly, after insistent and repeated warnings, exposed his helpless troops murderously to a surprise attack.

Overcoming the fury of his rage, he could calmly then announce:

"General St. Clair shall have justice. I looked hastily through the dispatches, saw the whole disaster but not all the particulars; I will receive him without displeasure; I will hear him without prejudice. He shall have justice."

Who, then will marvel at the words of Thomas Jefferson, written long after his break with Washington? "His integrity was most pure; his justice the most inflexible I have ever known. No motives of interest, consanguinity, friendship or hatred could bias his decision."

GREATEST OF MEN—WASHINGTON

Nations are accustomed to indulge the eccentricities of an illustrious or favored son. The affectations of the pomp-plagued and ambitious are readily forgiven. One nation has been robbed of an opportunity to exhibit its charity in forgiveness. Washington was utterly free from whim, caprice, and make-believe. He had neither window-dresser nor press-agent. There were no artificial needs in his life. The philosophy that teaches self-indulgence only to be followed by disillusionment, bitterness and despair he never tasted. Hence his inability to recognize morbidity or to comprehend the meaning of hopelessness.

Lashed by violent impulses and furious reactions, he suffered no complex unless worship of self-mastery can be included among this group of morbidities. A stranger to fear, he is not to be praised for exposing himself continuously to the hazards of a choice necessitated by his concept of honor, yet for the choice itself there can be nothing but acclaim.

CHAPTER XL

WASHINGTON AND THE MOB

IN all the crises that beset him, in which his own judgment had to be exercised upon the instant, he invariably acted as if the entire horizon lay before him on a platter. His few outstanding mistakes resulted through the surrender of his judgment after consulting with others. Yet many of his greatest achievements were due to his habit of declining to act alone when wise counsels were available.

Truth was the objective of his intellect; the objective of his will was good. To these objectives he brought the power of a personality unswayed by a distorted view of proportions or a motive unworthy of a churchman.

Aristocratic in all his tastes, he was democratic in all his aspirations. No man knew better the folly of planting a seed in gravel, expecting it to grow. Washington had no illusions concerning the mob. A hundred times the mob had failed him. Consequently he was not blind to the danger of permitting the mob to ride at random upon an unharnessed idea. Under the inspiration of integrity in high

GREATEST OF MEN—WASHINGTON

places he knew as well as Jefferson that the mob could always be trusted. But he also knew what Jefferson knew not so well—that when betrayed, deceived or disillusioned by those from whom the mob had a right to expect unsullied, even heroic, virtue, no man might foresee the extravagance or the extent of the mob's resentment. This vision alone, illuminated by faith in a Divine Providence, was sufficient to bring into his private and public life a standard of strict morality rarely encountered among the great ones of earth.

It was his sense of responsibility and his foreknowledge of the effect of his conduct upon a nation in the making that made him grave, even sombre, as the years went on.

His sense of humor was extraordinary, as his diary graphically reveals, and his penetration of the vanities, hypocrisies, self-interests and intrigues of many of his incompletely pedestalled contemporaries was so keen that he shrank from the outward show with unskillfully concealed disgust.

Estimating at its face value the emptiness of public acclaim, the insincerity of public display, the skin-deep significance of public pomp, he so hungered for simplicity that despite the difficulties of the long journey, he ran off from the artificial elegance of his state-life fifteen times during his eight years of office as President. He wanted to be with

WASHINGTON AND THE MOB

Martha alone at Mt. Vernon, and Martha, as his letter of May 4, 1794, to Mr. William Pearce, revealed, would not choose to be anywhere without him.

Reprobating coarseness of speech, he was so careful in his choice of words that in the thousands of written pages left behind him not one syllable of vulgarity can be found. Of his public correspondence alone Washington wrote more than two hundred volumes of folio manuscript. This is the quantity purchased by Congress. In addition there were thousands of private letters. Nobody will ever know the size of the heap burned by Martha, nor the number of thousands of pages torn from their moorings by Bushrod Washington and given by him as relics to the vast throngs who in the very earliest years, following the great man's death, began their pilgrimages to Mt. Vernon. The extent of his agricultural monographs can only be guessed at, for of these many hundreds of pages are still in existence. His household and plantation accounts, his expense memoranda and his diary notes, scarcely more than half of which have been preserved, require a score of volumes to give them shelter.

Yet we have been told that this man, who wrote more than Jefferson, Hamilton and Bancroft combined, found writing difficult; that he labored with his quill; that his thoughts tangled themselves so

GREATEST OF MEN—WASHINGTON

clumsily that only by the painful drudgery of erasures, deletions, interlineations and fresh beginnings could his hand unravel the knotted confusion of his brain.

Overwhelming is the evidence that for clarity, directness, precision, elegance and dignity his native gifts, untrained, were so great that only his greatness in far greater gifts, completely overshadowing the lesser, can explain the false opinions entertained upon this point by men capable of sounder judgment.

And the sum of all he wrote is so completely eclipsed by the sum of half he did that the modern critic must gasp in astonishment when contemplating the problem of how he found time for writing under the shadows of so much doing, or time for doing between the intervals of writing.

Moreover! There is the additional problem to stump and baffle, to confound and defeat the trained psychologist who professes to know the Human Mind. Who can understand Washington's failure throughout the enormous mass of his correspondence to make the slightest, the most trivial, the merest hint of reference to himself in connection with the influence he exerted upon the Virginia House of Burgesses, the Continental Congresses, the Revolution, the birth and fostering of the new nation?

Nowhere among his sentences can be found even

WASHINGTON AND THE MOB

a guarded allusion to any of his exploits, achievements, triumphs or defeats. With a thousand opportunities to indulge in cautious reminder of his own conception of his own greatness, never did he yield to the temptation. This profound evidence of his veneration of modesty, excluding all other testimony, is sufficient corroboration of Thomas Jefferson's tribute to the personal purity of his life. How often has such Modesty been seen upon the mountain peaks of the world?

CHAPTER XLI

OF FLESH AND FAITH

OF course he respected the dignity of his own person and could be satisfied only with the finest linens, silks and satins. Connoisseur and sensualist by nature, he indulged in all that was licit, but at the same time threw himself eagerly when duty commanded into prolonged and dreadful periods of hardship and privation.

His slaves were his "people," his officers his "family." Long before his death slavery worried him, and he poured out his soul on the subject a generation before the birth of Lincoln. Writing to General Alexander Spotwood, November 23, 1794, he said:

"With respect to the other species of property, I shall frankly declare to you that I do not like even to think, much less to talk of it.—However, as you have put the question, I shall, in a few words, give my ideas of it. Were it not that I am principalled against selling negroes, as you would do cattle at a market, I would not, in twelve months from this date, be possessed of one as a slave.—I shall be happily mistaken, if they are not found to be a very

OF FLESH AND FAITH

troublesome species of property ere many years pass over our heads."

Little straining is required to make this look like a prophesy of the Civil War. To David Stuart he wrote, February 7, 1796, revealing his anxiety in brooding over the inevitable pangs of separation which he clearly foresaw in the freedom he even then was planning for his human chattels, a freedom for which he made provision in his will.

He must rent, farm out or sell his slaves. The only other alternative is freedom. "Quite enough it will be when it is considered how much the Dower Negroes and my own are intermarried, and the former with the neighboring Negroes, to part whom will be an affecting and trying affair, happen when it will."

Unashamed to fall upon his knees in audible prayer at the bedside of a dying child, who will say he did not kneel at Valley Forge? Here tradition, fathered by the simple statement of a common soldier, assumes the dignity of historic fact.

Believing with the simple faith of a child that God is on his side, and confronted by the necessity of Providential intervention when the sky is without a single star and all about him are in despair, the one thing to expect of such a man is to find him on his knees.

GREATEST OF MEN—WASHINGTON

Stressing the depth of his faith, Washington wrote the Reverend Dr. William Gordon, October 15, 1797, two years before his death:

"Rural employments while I am spared, which in the natural course of things cannot be long, will now take place of toil—responsibility—and the solicitudes attending the walks of public life;—and with vows for the peace, the happiness & prosperity of a country in whose service the prime of my life hath been spent,—and with best wishes for the tranquility of all Nations, and all men, the scene will close; grateful to that Providence which hath directed my steps & shielded me in the various changes & chances through which I have passed, from my youth to the present moment."

He was not a poet. Businessmen rarely browse at the foothills of Parnassus; never ascend the slope. Washington was an executive, a leader, a creator. He could inspire poetry and feel it, but he could not sing. He could manage a House of Burgesses, two Congresses, a Constitutional Convention, a tatterdemalion army, a Revolutionary War, a new government brought into existence without a model, a Cabinet to make it go. But he could also manage a fishery, a flour mill, a whiskey still, five tobacco plantations, five grain farms, a score of shops devoted to weaving, harness-making, carpentering, smithing, butchering, baking, and dairying.

OF FLESH AND FAITH

He could rotate crops scientifically and foretell a system of transportation by steam to carry his crops to market. Fond of plum cake and Madeira, a noble homestead and luxurious environment, he was content with salt cod, corn bread, honey, cherry bounce, a tall horse, a camp fire, a bed of leaves and no cover between himself and the sky but his own cloak. The day before he was bled to death he spent five hours in the saddle.

Not all the allurements of Europe's frenzy of enthusiasm for the man Europe looked upon as the forerunner and counterpart of its own Napoleon could tempt him to cross the Atlantic to receive the adulations which his march of triumph would have brought like a crown of glory upon his head. Washington was not a worshipper of pedigrees. Knowing that his ancestors were met upon their arrival by men of coppery complexion who had preceded the original 100 per cent. American white by thousands of years, he did not boast of an ancestry reaching down into the roots of culture, achievement and social distinction.

So little did he care about his own pedigree that he never took the trouble to learn the full name of his own grandfather, remaining in ignorance of it until his death. May 18, 1794, he wrote Robert Lewis, his nephew . . .

GREATEST OF MEN—WASHINGTON

"The title papers are not to be found; nor the manner in which my mother came by it to be traced with precision. I have understood it was left to her by her father, but what his Christian name was, I am unable to tell you, nor the County he lived in with certainty, but presume it was Lancaster."

Of individual worthiness Washington thought not of the things a man's ancestors might have done but of the things a man himself does. Upstarts were quickly appraised by this keen and withering judge. Under ten words and a smile he could hide a chapter of scorn. His classic to Gouverneur Morris is swollen with mirthful contempt:

"They are not bad in giving themselves a good character."

Another and less compassionate phase of his contempt for knavery could not be so smugly confined. Addressing himself to the profiteers of the Revolution, he could write a paragraph, to the sting of which too few gave heed in the great war of 1914:

"It is much to be lamented, that each State long ere this has not hunted them down as pests to society, and the greatest enemies we have to the happiness of America. I would to God, that some one of the most atrocious in each State was hung in gibbets upon a gallows five times as high as the one pre-

OF FLESH AND FAITH

pared for Haman. No punishment, in my opinion, is too great for the man, who can build his greatness upon his country's ruin."

If this is the ruthlessness of the man of flesh it is offset by the affectionate tenderness and sweetness of his happy sentiments toward the younger Lafayette, whose vivacity, freshness, unselfishness, courage and unashamed love, in the midst of harrowing trials, afforded the great warrior an inexhaustible source of consolation and renewed confidence in human nature.

CHAPTER XLII

WHO'S WHO IN AMERICA

NEITHER was there lineage of royalty behind him, nor could he see before him quite as far as the twentieth century offspring of "Who's Who in America." In making this assertion the writer intends no envious sneer. It serves merely to lift Washington above the charge that he was an aristocrat without knowing that aristocracy, in its truest sense, is the bud, blossom and flower of democracy, the idolized dream, aspiration, and hope of every democratic cradle.

Wholly lacking in vanity, his pictures, multiplied during his lifetime by hundreds, could look like or unlike him. He cared little for the effigy.

The important beginning of each new day for Washington at home or on the road was the rising sun. That he might be able to greet the solar orb with a fresh heart, no gaiety of social life could keep him out of bed after nine o'clock.

Gentle, firm, temperate, patient, long-suffering, brave beyond human understanding, just, generous, charitable, wise, noble, gallant, elegant, he loved to ride with "Jacky," to dance "Jacky's" sister on his knee, to plant shrubbery and tree, to chase a fox that could elude him, to come home with or without a duck, to drop into the store at Alexandria to send "a lot of things up to the house," to provide medical attention for the sick, to keep a store of pork and grain for those standing in need of it, to leave a tip for old Granny, to send for double-width blankets of the best quality for his slaves who are teasing him for them.

Could a harsh and forbidding master, of whom his slaves were in awe, write to his intimate and affectionate friend, Tobias Lear, as Washington wrote him, September 7, 1791?

Lear lived at Mt. Vernon and knew the ease and familiarity of Washington's relations with his family. Could anything be more absurd or stupid than a letter to one who knew all his secrets, falsely setting forth such a hypocritical proposal as "send them down by the first vessel which is bound to Alexandria as my negroes are all teasing me for them & the season will soon make them necessary"?

There was nothing to conceal from Tobias Lear. December 12, 1794, Washington instructed him in writing to rummage his presses and trunks at Mt. Vernon for papers respecting the transactions of the Directors of the Potomac Company. Had there been secrets to conceal Washington could not have written:

GREATEST OF MEN—WASHINGTON

"Mrs. Fanny Washington has the master key of all the others (presses and trunks) from whom you can get it, but whether the papers are to be found in the press or in any Trunks I am unable to inform you;—the keys of the locked trunks are, if I remember rightly, in my writing Table; the key of which remains in it."

In other words, the doors were open. The key was in the lock. All the other keys were behind the lock. There were no secrets.

Washington must have had faults. Who cares to put them under a microscope? Like the faint pock marks on his countenance, not many of them deep, they but served to sublimate the simple beauty of his spirit, stressing in their littleness the bigness of the contrast, making men who came after him by more than a hundred years lift their hats in reverence at the mention of his name.

Few indeed are the dead who can inspire love in the hearts of the living, and here lies the most extraordinary phenomenon in the life and death of Washington, the man. The more one seeks to touch the tomb in which all that is mortal of him remains, the more one's heart beats warmly for having come so close to something so utterly worthy of love.

A simple spirit! Washington abhorred extravagance. "Neat and plain" he demanded of his secretary, specifying the character of the house the president should live in. "Not by any means in an extravagant style; because the latter is not only contrary to my wishes, but would, in reality, be repugnant to my interest and convenience."

But what about the innuendo respecting the awkward letters he wrote, making excuses for his unwillingness to lend money to people in difficult circumstances? He was always lending money, and few knew, because he refused to occupy the presidential mansion at the expense of the public, how frequently he was embarrassed by reason of poverty. "One of the wealthiest men of America" was land poor. Easily understood is his letter of May 6, 1794, to his secretary—a secretary who knew the truth:

"For altho' in the estimation of the world, I possess a good and clear estate, yet so unproductive is it (through the neglect of nearly twenty years) that I am oftentimes ashamed to refuse aids which I cannot afford, unless I was to sell part of it to answer the purposes. Besides these I have another motive which makes me earnestly wish for these things—it is indeed more powerful than all the rest—namely to liberate a certain species of property (slaves) which I possess very repugnantly to my own feelings; but which imperious necessity compels."

Ever desiring to tread on sure ground and conscious of the significance of his own native simplicity, he would enter Philadelphia to take up his duties as president in an old coach. He thanks Mr. Page for offering to send his new coach to meet him at Chester, "but as it is my wish & intention to enter the City without any parade or notice, the old Coach will answer the purpose of the New One."

Charity and forbearance are to be expected from such a man, and we are not surprised to find him patiently tolerating a worthless white man, a negligent overseer whose bad qualities and bad example would induce Washington to look out for a successor to him were it not for the poor creature's unfortunate family.

"His idling and drinking grow worse and worse, in consequence whereof he dares not find fault with those who are entrusted to his care lest they should retort and disclose his rascally conduct." Rather than ruin the man's family by discharging him, Washington accepts promise after promise from him only to discover that no sort of reliance or dependence can be reposed upon the ungrateful fellow. So he says, May 4, 1794:

"By which means work that the same number of hands would perform in a week takes mine a month. —Nothing but compassion for his helpless family, has hitherto induced me to keep him a moment in my service, so bad is the example he sets."

WHO'S WHO IN AMERICA

In the sense that we are all sinners, Washington was a sinner. In the sense that he was made in the image and likeness of God there shines from the record of his life, from all its many sides, a light that brings those who see it clearly just a little closer to their Maker. As Washington could see God in Christ, so can lesser men see in Washington the handiwork of God.

CHAPTER XLIII

WASHINGTON AND YOUTH

WHAT does George Washington mean to the youth of this stormy generation? In what manner does this man of faith, hope, love and courage speak to the America he made?

We have been leading a hectic life—a complex life—a life of sapping luxuries, futile artificialities and selfish competitions. Our highest purposes have been swallowed by a devouring industrial monster. A philosophy of materialism has engulfed us. Morbidity frowns behind so many human acts that once were free and spontaneous.

Youth sees that millions of boys can be sent to slaughter by a civilization whose mightiest achievements in chemistry, physics, electricity, metallurgy and statesmanship serve only to make war all the more terrible. To youth such a civilization, debasing all its arts and sciences, seems to lead to ruin. Certainly it leads to disillusionment and disgust, to skepticism and cynicism, to bitterness and despair. Youth cannot be expected to know the world as it is. Its own small experience constitutes the only world within its comprehension. In vain does youth

WASHINGTON AND YOUTH

turn to its professors of psychology and higher criticism. In vain does it turn to science. In its confusion and perplexity it would be indeed stupid to turn for reassurance to religion. Science knows nothing of religion. Man as a mere piece of mechanism can have no possible need of religion. Religion is out of fashion. All the old orthodoxy about stealing other men's property and other men's wives and all the old moral codes were so much mummery to be abandoned with the emancipation of intellect.

How terribly intellect has failed! Its effort to explain the heart hunger and the baffling aspirations of man throughout his history is so muddled, so futile, and life led by intellect alone is so utterly purposeless. Without purpose there can be no beauty, no ideal, no truth, no objective of mind or will.

Of course there are books and contradictions and refutations and more books and more contradictions. Of course theories are espoused and discarded in the same breath. The problems of youth remain unsolved because with premature weariness of a very ugly and a very soulless world they become all the more insoluble.

If youth has been blighted we can lay the blight to materialism. If man is only an automotive machine why should he struggle at all? His very capacity for pleasure is lessened, not increased, by indulgence. Satiety is barren. Where the one and only and inevitable factor is death why postpone release from predominating evil? Why not speed up the pace for a brief flare and when the spurt begins to falter end it all?

Of a certainty there is no faith where there can be none. Love is but a biochemic reaction. The idealism of fidelity and devotion between man and woman can be neither pure nor sacred where the sexes are no more than self-perpetuating appetites. Happiness is a chimera—an empty shell. Belief in eternity, in heaven, in God is reserved for oldish women as Santa Claus for infants. Distrusting its own reactions to the environment in which it exists, how can youth trust a revelation which its fathers have abandoned? How absurd are dogma and spiritual contemplations when spirit itself is discovered to be an elaboration of deceit. No, the fragments of shallow sentimentality coming over from a dead past cannot submit themselves to the cold scrutiny of a mechanistic philosophy and expect to survive.

Washington knew little of public schools, nothing of colleges. Modern industry had not been born when, that day before his death, sleet-soaked and weary, he dropped out of his saddle at Mt. Vernon and turned his horse toward the barn he was never

WASHINGTON AND YOUTH

to see again. There was little science in the world when Washington came into it, and scarcely more when he went out of it. Chemistry was still in the web of alchemy. Physics had scarcely been applied, except to the wheel and the bar.

Psychoanalysis had not yet formulated its lofty phrases. Religion was still a reality. Ministers of the gospel, Baptists, Presbyterians, Lutherans, Anglicans, Catholics, Jews were still looked upon as honest men. There was no Sinclair Lewis to defame all ministers as dishonest men. The very fact that as intelligent beings they could have made more money then, as they can now, in some worldly occupation than in the pulpit and yet were led to the pulpit by an urge they could not resist was proof of their honesty of purpose even though their opinions might be warped.

The age of Washington would have resented a Sinclair Lewis assault against the ministers of the gospel as something obviously evil, something too transparent in its morbidity to be tolerated by the most outspoken enemy of religion.

Washington, as we have seen, has been accused of despising religion. Yet we have also seen him appealing in his desperation for a chaplain. We know he had no Gantry complex. He was a big, warm, generous, just, courageous and chivalrous figure of a man. Ah, yes. But he was too simple,

GREATEST OF MEN—WASHINGTON

too primitive, too much a part of the unperplexed conventions of his dull and vegetative age to be tormented by any of the bewildering riddles that now plague this sophisticated twentieth century.

What, then, can a dead Washington out of a past that no longer exists mean to a generation so far advanced in sophistry that scores of college students can find no way out of its stifling miasma except through suicide?

Are the schools of which Washington knew so little, and which Al Smith loves so much, responsible for the present state of affairs? What was the theory upon which they were founded? How have they departed from that theory? If they have defects, are the young to blame?

These are questions before which Washington's defamers may well tremble. Most of us accept the proposition that the American schools were founded to perpetuate the representative system of local government in each of the United States by convincing their pupils of the wisdom, prudence, far-sighted vision and sanity of the fathers. They teach patriotism, love of country, devotion to the flag, equal opportunity to all. The citizen looks upon them, to use the words of John W. Burke,

"as representing the unchanging American tradition from the founding of the government but is un-

WASHINGTON AND YOUTH

mindful of the radical changes introduced among them during the last several generations. This severance from the past has permitted in recent years the development of a school of thought unsympathetic with the principles upon which the American government was established. It is bearing fruit in unwise legislation. Many educated men and women now advocate centralized direct action, which always has been the governmental method of Europe whether monarchist or bolshevist."

This development has been fostered despite the warnings of Washington, who saw in the European system all the seeds of decay and death. The Washington government was evolved, as Burke clearly points out,

"by intellectual giants through a process of pure reasoning, and it never can be understood by the average youth or adult without intelligent instruction by teachers who themselves thoroughly understand it. Unwise instruction may indeed produce a patriotic zeal which, ignorant of the true principles of government, would strive to improve it by mutilation. A better understanding of our original system of government can be obtained only by looking at the political nostrums of this day through the same lens our fathers used. These nostrums, put forth as a new panacea, were old and stale when they were first carefully examined and discarded during those trying months in the Constitutional Convention of 1787.

"Our children today have no more to do with the

new thought, the new freedom, than a feather with the wind. They are subject to forces which they cannot see and do not understand, directed upon them by ourselves and they are reacting normally as they might be expected to react."

Washington was not primitive. He is not out of date. We might as well say that the multiplication table is primitive and out of date. Washington was a modern. He was surrounded by moderns, the most farseeing and enlightened in our history. He was their inspiration and their leader. His problems were terrific, appalling, well-nigh hopeless. He met them with courage, with faith in God, with dependence upon a force higher than any he himself could control or command. He met them sanely, nobly, gloriously. He sought not his own personal welfare but the welfare of generations to come, the very generation in which we ourselves flounder by reason of indifference to the principles which to him were the most sacred and enduring of humanity's long and troubled history.

Smartly we skim over the surface of that tremendous struggle and count its ripples without a thought of peering into its depths. Washington, aflame with love and lovable beyond any other character of his own century or ours, wise, serene, capable, good, unselfish, human and humane, reaches out to the youth of this distracted hour with the solici-

WASHINGTON AND YOUTH

tude of a father for his child. His message to youth is not to be received in a capsule. There is nothing abstract or academic about it. We who are no longer children must go to the man himself and listen to him. We must sit at his feet and kneel at his side and follow where he leads—into temperance, tolerance, charity, integrity, purity of motive, purity of life; we must follow him to the God in whom our silver dollars still remind us we trust.

Old-fashioned? Calvin Coolidge standing at a window of the White House can look out and say: "I see the monument still stands." Who today among statesmen is so sane, so honest, so direct? Yes, we need him now. We need his idealism and his courage, his readiness to surrender personal comfort, his readiness to put his riches into jeopardy, his readiness to reject ambition and the lure of worldly honor. What nation has been blessed with greater inspiration? Where, then, is Washington? Why have we allowed him to become a name to be perfunctorily honored once a year with wreaths and a holiday? Why are we content to know as little of him as our school histories hurriedly exhibit?

The dead Washington is not Washington at all. It is the man, the living man, the great and just and good man, who would give back to youth the priceless treasures stolen from its soul.

CHAPTER XLIV

WASHINGTON—THE MAN'S MAN

WASHINGTON'S reaction upon posterity is scarcely to be measured. His reaction upon the world of his own day was tremendous. Men actually plotted against each other to get closer to him. Nations plunged into orgies of extravagance in striving to follow what they thought, for the moment, was his example. Yet they never truly comprehended his example, for he was the one foolproof great man of history.

Indeed his possession of so many unique qualities has made it difficult in the extreme for mimic statesmen to exhibit successfully a counterfeit presentment of the original. These same qualities have defied the cartoonist to set him forth in caricature. The *London Punch*, between May 11, 1861, and February 18, 1865, repeatedly succeeded in cartooning "Abe Lincoln." Its one effort, January 10, 1863, to cartoon Washington resulted in a figure of ghostly but majestic dignity which completely baffled the skill of the artist, rendering his ridicule abortive.

Small imitators inspired by a great model invariably go as far as their natural limitations permit

WASHINGTON—THE MAN'S MAN

and then, vainly trying to mount higher than their genius enables them to climb, they totter and fall into excesses and oblivion.

The upstart may utilize what appears to be the instrumentalities and methods of his inspiration, but usually, because the shadow is not and never can be the substance, he bungles at the first crisis, thereby begetting other crises which eventually swallow him. Conscience would avert the bungling but conscience is one of the tools not always used.

What Washington succeeded in doing in America produced a terrific impression upon the young Napoleon, who, if he ever had a conscience, found it a menace to his dreams. Perhaps it was not the young Napoleon's fault that, although he possessed many of the tools which Washington would have declined to use had they been available, he lacked the very tools that made Washington's work possible. Washington began with an upheaval of his own making; Napoleon found an upheaval already prepared for him. Washington managed his upheaval conscientiously for the benefit of men; Napoleon, without conscience, tried to manage men for the benefit of himself.

The misuse of Washington's tools and the distortion of the significance of Washington's achievements made the dictator possible—for a time. The lapse of a century makes possible—for a time—the successor of Napoleon, Mussolini. Had Napoleon been less a lover of self or had he been, like Washington, a lover of men the subsequent history of Europe might easily have made the World War impossible.

Autocracies and dictatorships, exhibiting themselves under whatsoever name, would have perished in Europe at the hands of Napoleon as they perished in America at the hands of Washington had Napoleon adequately appraised the true character of the Mt. Vernon farmer.

The Washington model disillusioned ambitious men on the American side of the Atlantic, making them realize that to whatsoever heights their exaggerated dreams of power might soar an offsetting and neutralizing idea had been born in the hearts of Washington's people, making it impossible henceforth forever for an adventurer or a dictator to flourish among them for an hour. Herbert Hoover, who had been food dictator in Belgium, discreetly changed his title to food administrator in the United States.

Washington dealt with love; Napoleon with hate. Thus far in the career of Mussolini no man is justified in attempting to identify the nature of the raw material upon which he works. Washington was a mixture of soldier and man. Napoleon was a mixture of soldier and politician. Mussolini,

WASHINGTON—THE MAN'S MAN

as far as we know, is politician only, but he thinks of soldiers and speaks in reverence of Cæsar.

Washington made it impossible for the mixture of soldier and politician to endure in America, yet in forever warning the rest of the world against this showy but ephemeral and devastating combination he brought about no stupendous calamity. On the contrary he stressed the human value of sanity, order, religion and peace in terms of men, freedom, property and progress.

Europe to this hour has taken no advantage of his warning and has rarely heeded the significance of his demonstration.

Older and more experienced, Europe has strangely chosen the sword of Damocles seemingly unconscious that the sword is never used, except to destroy, and that its power of destruction is so great that just as frequently it falls upon him who wields as upon the intended victim.

Perhaps Washington is too far off to influence Mussolini, but between Washington and Mussolini lies the dead body of the self-crowned Napoleon, beside him the record in blood of the hundred preventable wars that have sapped Europe since his death. History is crammed with tarnished glamour and faded illusions. America has her vices, but Washington, freeing her mind from all fetters, made it possible in a single century for all the recessive

GREATEST OF MEN—WASHINGTON

factors of the human intellect to come out of the repressions of ages to blossom and flower and fructify. Pure science and applied science have leaped from this freedom in America and even in haltered Europe the American overflow has stimulated the gathering of an enormous harvest.

As far as the physical comforts of the plain people are involved America is a thousand years ahead of Europe. Granted that Europe still possesses the tarnished glamour and the faded illusions, she also possesses the very system that leads to more tarnished glamour and more faded illusions.

Europe never had a Washington, and Mussolini, however important his achievements, for the time, in his own Italy, nowhere seems to resemble Washington, so that the distorted and mutilated influences which have come to Mussolini by way of Napoleon from Washington promise little for Europeans.

Who among the great ones of Europe can be thought of at this hour as a man's man? How else can we think of Washington? In that simple phrase "a man's man," is there not more hope and more promise for this very tired and very crazy world than is to be found in any other phrase with which mankind is familiar?

And what is a man's man? Look at Washington calmly, with all his animal impulses in harness and all his faculties of mind, heart and body de voted to the welfare of men with no petty reserva tions for himself. Look at him unashamed not onl as a man of men but as a man of God. Does h not answer the question? If so, is not America he self in danger by reason of her growing sophist cation? In a sense Washington cannot be up-to date because he was not sophisticated. Europe ha ever been sophisticated and the very blindness o her sophistication has kept her from seeing Wasl ington—from recognizing what Washington woul mean to her if she could see him.

Indeed, has she not made a systematic effort t keep the image of Washington hidden from he people? What European of power is ready to su render power? What European of might has eve undertaken to emulate the example of Washington Truly may it be said that Washington is not know in Europe, except among the few who have n means of making him known to the many. Tru also may it be said that even in America—in tl America he made—there is a tendency to forget th man's man—this greatest of men.

THE END

www.ingramcontent.com/pod-product-compliance
Lightning Source LLC
Chambersburg PA
CBHW050341230426
43663CB00010B/1945